The Infinite Power

Within

Unbind Your Mind
& Ascend To Freedom

The Infinite Power
Within

---

*Unbind Your Mind
& Ascend To Freedom*

Lorie Gannon

Quantity discounts are available on bulk orders.
Contact info@TAGPublishers.com for more information.

TAG Publishing, LLC
2618 S. Lipscomb
Amarillo, TX 79109
www.TAGPublishers.com

Office (806) 373-0114
Fax (806) 373-4004
info@TAGPublishers.com

ISBN: 978-1-59930-395-6

First Edition

Dedication

My dear son, you are my life and I love you beyond what words can express.

Because of this book, I am a better parent. Your life is anything and everything you want it to be. Go out there and do it!

I sincerely want to thank all my LifeSuccess colleagues whom I met at the training summit. Each and every one of you has enriched my life in a very special way. More importantly, each and every one of you has generously supported me in writing this book. I will forever be grateful to you.

I want to thank my coach, Mark Moffitt, for welcoming me onto the LifeSuccess Consulting team. It has been a pleasure to know you, to work with you, and most of all, to get to know myself better through your guidance. I hope to work with you on many more projects and business ventures in the future.

About the Author

Lorie Gannon is an entrepreneur and speaker who believes in infinite self expansion. She is dedicated to inspiring and educating people on how to expand their lives beyond boundaries. Lorie motivates everyone she meets to follow their goals and strive to be their personal best. She understands the value of releasing fear and focusing on all that life has to offer.

Fluent in both English and French, Lorie graduated with distinction from McGill University with a Bachelor of Commerce. A successful financial advisor for the past 15 years, Lorie has received numerous promotions and accolades. Along with her financial savvy, Lorie is also an accomplished pianist, who took classical piano lessons for almost a decade and successfully passed the annual exams at the Montreal Conservatory of Music. Lorie's unparalleled work in the field of personal development has given way to launching her own coaching business and speaking engagements. Though she is involved in various business endeavors, Lorie always makes time for her son. Her commitment to her family and clients is a testament to her own purpose and passion for cultivating greatness in others.

Foreword

Lorie Gannon knows why she was put on this earth; she knows her purpose. But that wasn't always the case. In her mid thirties, frustrated with mediocre results, fearful, tired of sitting on the sidelines, and admiring others for their success, she made a decision that led her to a path of personal development that changed her life.

2011 will mark 50 years from the day I picked up Napoleon Hill's classic, *Think and Grow Rich*. I've been a serious student of the mind and have spent virtually all of my adult life studying human behavior: why we do the things we do and don't do some of the things we know will bring us better results. We have deep reservoirs of potential lying dormant within and all we need is the key to unlock it. *The Infinite Power Within* is the key we've been looking for.

We all want to explore our dreams and live an abundant life but so many are too afraid to do so. Lorie however is just the opposite. She is a striking example of what's possible when you make an irrevocable decision to step out of your comfort zone and go for your dreams. Today, Lorie lives the way she wants to live rather than how other people want her to. *The Infinite Power Within* provides us with tools to reach our goals and follow our ideals. Lorie's valuable knowledge and experience will help steer you in the direction of your dreams.

The freedom to make sound decisions based on what we really want is vital to our success. When we relinquish our fear and choose our thoughts, rather than live by default, we put ourselves in a position to unleash our real power within and begin to create the life we want. Lorie takes a proactive approach and sets an example for all she meets.

The Infinite Power Within teaches us in straightforward language how to overcome our fears, remove doubt, move beyond obstacles, and take charge of our lives. There's nothing complicated about it... it starts with a decision. Lorie's heartfelt stories along with her words of encouragement offer the right combination of teaching and inspiration to help you achieve your life long goals. Success is within the reach of every person no matter their background or circumstance and Lorie Gannon is proof positive.

–Bob Proctor, Teacher in The Secret and
best selling author of *You Were Born Rich*

Table of Contents

Introduction..13

Chapter One: What Are You Afraid Of?............................21

Chapter Two: Who's in Control?.......................................41

Chapter Three: Unlocking the Mysteries of the Majestic Mind..59

Chapter Four: Harvest Your Thoughts..............................81

Chapter Five: Purpose: The Starting Point for All Achievements...99

Chapter Six: What Do You Really Want?.......................117

Chapter Seven: Defy Your Comfort Zone.......................137

Chapter Eight: A Whole New World................................153

Chapter Nine: Conquer the War Within..........................169

Chapter Ten: Freedom! The Other Side of Fear.............185

Introduction

In life, we can only go as far as our fears. When I considered writing a book for the first time, I became immersed in a complex mix of emotions: resistance, fear of disappointment, fear of failure, indecision, and doubt, to name a few. However, if I think back on how the story of my becoming a published author unfolded—and believe me, I think about it every day—I regain confidence that the most rewarding experiences happen in our lives when we are able to let go and have faith. The positive reinforcement at the end is priceless. This has been the case with *The Infinite Power Within*. This book "came to me," as opposed to my deliberately seeking it out.

At the onset of my journey, I spent a great deal of time thinking that in my mid-thirties, I should be enjoying a much higher level of success in the areas of happiness, health and wealth. I was far from having reached my ambitions, and found that I could no longer accept the status quo. I was tired of sitting in the sidelines, admiring others for their success: I wanted it for myself. How could I bridge this gap? I tried a few things here and there, obtaining temporary improvements— but they never lasted. When I started to examine my life, I came to understand why. I was focusing on external changes: jobs, boyfriends, diets, clothing, hobbies—you name it. But I came to the realization that the outside is but a reflection of the inside, meaning I would have to reach deep inside myself to change who I was—a notion that terrified me. I needed to find some answers.

One day, I reviewed the website of Bob Proctor, a highly-regarded authority in the personal development industry with impressive expertise on the subject of understanding the mind. Bob's work had always fascinated me, so when I came across the opportunity to join his international team of consultants, I decided to enroll. I figured this would grant me the privilege of working in close partnership with him, and at the same time, give my life a new direction. As I studied his materials and started to understand the power of the mind, I felt reborn and driven by a new vitality. I became so passionate about this life-changing information that it led me to discover my life purpose: to help people who want to change their lives for the better and enjoy lasting happiness.

Several months later, I attended the summit held at the Marriott Hotel in Delray Beach Florida, where I was completing the training program to become a certified LifeSuccess Consultant. Among the various speakers we had the privilege of hearing at the summit was a representative from LifeSuccess Publishing. Just before he addressed us, Bob Proctor presented to us the reasons we should all seriously consider writing our own book. Even then, I acknowledged that there were several important benefits to writing a book, especially in that doing so could rapidly move my business to a whole new level.

However, I didn't feel a strong calling to write a book. It was not part of my short- or medium-term business plans, and I thought I had more pressing business development needs to attend to. At the end of the presentation, we were told that there were publishing contracts available should anyone in the room be interested in meeting to discuss this opportunity at greater length. Some people rushed quickly to make an appointment. I rose slowly, waited for the crowd to subside, and then decided to make an appointment more out of curiosity than out of a genuine personal interest. I intentionally made my appointment as late in the week as possible in order to give myself a chance to reconsider my decision to meet to discuss the possibility of a book.

The following day, while we were sent on a quick break, I grabbed the opportunity to ask Bob a question. After answering me, he looked at me and said, "So, are you going to do it?" "Do what?" I asked. "Write your book," he replied. "Well, I don't know Bob ... I am not sure this is something I want to pursue. But just in case, I made an appointment on Friday." He looked at me with a smile and said, "Good!" When our training day came to an end and my colleagues got ready to move to the next room to have dinner, I decided to go up to my room to freshen up, and to call my son to get some news. When I was finished, I went back to join my colleagues for dinner. All of a sudden, my coach Mark came up to me and asked, "Where were you? Bob was looking for you?" I replied that I was just coming back from my room. "Bob has found the title for your book," Mark said, handing me a sheet of paper that read, "The Other Side of Fear." I was speechless. Mark took me to where Bob was sitting, and I said to him, "Wow, Bob! That is a great idea! I am deeply touched! The more I think about the idea of writing a book, the more I like it." That night, I went to bed in a state of complete astonishment. Why did Bob think of *me* for this title? And why that specific title?

The next day, after returning to the seminar from another quick break, I happened to notice a copy of the publishing agreement lying on the table. By that time, some of my colleagues had met to discuss writing a book, and I guessed that someone had left their copy behind. Very curious, I decided to take a quick glance at the agreement to look at some of the terms and conditions. When I got to the last page and I saw the cost of the contract, I was stunned by the investment it represented. I found the numbers completely out of reach. Not only did I lack the amount of money required, but even if I wanted to write a book one day, it would take me years to accumulate such a sum of money. I placed the agreement back on the table. I did not want those numbers to influence in any way my upcoming meeting, which was the following day. Immediately after, a thought crossed my mind. There is no logical explanation for it, but the thought was: *The money is there.* I decided to have complete faith and trust in that thought. A little later during the day, I grabbed Bob again to ask him a question about money. I explained to him that I saw the cost of the publishing contract. I wanted to find a way to see beyond the numbers and focus my attention on making this opportunity a reality.

Bob described to me what he called the Law of Relativity. He explained just as one number can be big relative to a smaller number, everything else is relative too. For example, $10,000 is big relative to $1,000. Bob explained how rather than working from small to big, I should be working from big to small, so that the amount required for the book contract would become relatively small, and, as a result, more accessible, and more attainable. His explanation helped give me some perspective: that I should not treat the expense of writing this book as an obstacle. After answering my question, Bob decided to make a call right beside me. To my surprise, he called to request a design for the book cover of *The Other Side of Fear*—with my name on it. He asked to have the designs sent to him as quickly as possible. How could I not be breathless?

A few hours later, while we were almost at the end of our fourth training day, Bob received two cover designs and showed them to our group on the projecting screen. My heart almost stopped. What a feeling to see a book taking form right before your eyes... The designs were striking, such powerful depictions of the title. The book had not even been written, I had not yet had my meeting about the book contract, and yet it seemed that *The Other Side of Fear* was being born. I felt perplexed. What was happening, and why?

As we wrapped up our day, we headed for our last supper as a group. It was served to us in a very special setting, family-style. My colleague, Norman, sat beside me at the table. I was glad to have him by my side; we had shared some special moments together during the week and we were going to be enjoying another fabulous meal in one another's company. He turned to me and asked if I was going to get involved with a book deal. I said that I was leaning more and more toward it. "In that case, we have to start selling your book now!" he responded. Before I had a chance to ask what he meant, he told me to find a sheet of paper and write "Order Form" on the top of the page. He took the paper and went from person to person and from table to table, asking everyone to commit to buying my book, marking down the quantity of their choice and asking them to sign the form.

I could not believe my eyes. I would have never had the courage to take such an initiative myself, and here was Norman turning into my publishing agent! By the time he had gone across the room and asked everybody to sign the order form, 517 copies of my book were pre-sold! I was astounded. But more than anything else, I had been transported beyond my comfort zone, challenged to venture into the unknown.

I knew nothing about writing a book, not to mention paying for it. I was beginning to dread my meeting the next day. With everything that had taken place, how could I rain on the parade by shying away from this opportunity? How could I disappoint all of my colleagues, who had already manifested their support? I went to bed profoundly overwhelmed, not having the slightest notion of what my next step would be.

The next day at 1:00 pm, I had my meeting about the book contract. As far as I was from being ready to make such a high-stakes decision, I felt "guided" to do it. There was this powerful voice surging in me, saying, "Lorie, this is your way." I was so nervous. I took the initiative to start the discussion, and presented my offer first. I looked at the publishing representative straight in the eye, not blinking once, and I said to him that as things stood, I did not have the money to pay the first deposit. I explained to him that by signing an agreement for this book, he was actually signing one of his most lucrative publishing contracts ever. I wanted him to accept the 517 pre-sold copies of my book as the first deposit. That was all I had. I asked him bluntly: are you willing to do business with me? He was silent for a few seconds. At that point, I did not know how this would turn out. He looked at me and said that he was willing to accept my proposal. We worked out the remaining details of the agreement from there. I was ecstatic, but I was also one step closer to having no choice but to write this book.

Letting this opportunity slip through my fingers would have been a big mistake, something I would have no doubt regretted. The title alone was such an accurate representation of my life, most of which I had lived on the side of fear. I realized how many of my ideas had never flourished, how many opportunities I had lost, and how many of my important life goals had remained unfulfilled. It was time for a new day.

With everything that is going on in my life right now, I have all the reason in the world to continue living on the side of fear. However, the difference now is that I am learning to overcome my fears. I am a single mother with a 4-year-old child. I am planning a major career transition: I am starting my own business in personal development. I have recently purchased a new home of which I am the sole owner. I am writing a book. I am experiencing varying degrees of discomfort with all of these changes, forcing me to confront my insecurities. However, the adrenaline these changes create propels me even further, pushing me to surpass myself, to discover my true nature and my unique gifts. I feel every cell of my body vibrating. I feel alive. I feel I am growing.

As I advance in this project, I am focusing on all the positive aspects of writing this book. As a result, my ideas are flowing in abundance. I am opening myself to receive all that life has to offer, while letting go of my need to be in control of everything all the time. I know with certainty that this book will be a great success.

Fear is the resistance we experience in the face of an impending decision. We feel that we are in danger of losing something. By putting those emotions aside and attempting to look at a situation from a different perspective, it is possible to discover other ways of seeing it. As we expand our horizons, we give ourselves more choices. We move away from our tunnel vision. We see possibilities. This gives us hope and hope allows us to build a stronger faith. Faith eliminates fear. If I had let my fear be in control, this book would definitely not exist. I am blessed with this amazing opportunity to express myself, but most importantly, to reach, touch and change the lives of millions of people who continue to be immobilized by fear. My greatest gift is to teach people to unbind their mind and ascend to freedom.

While writing this book, I experienced several life-altering moments which accelerated the pace of my growth. As my life was transformed, the author in me evolved as well and I needed to reconsider the title of my book. I toyed with many different ideas other than *The Other Side of Fear* until one day, I sat down in front of my computer, closed my eyes and invoked the power of inspiration by saying "Spirit, please help me find my new title." And so *The Infinite Power Within* was born. This title reflected a continual progress that extends itself above and beyond this multifaceted adversary we call fear. Fear is the common denominator in many of the personal stories I share in this book; however, I didn't want to limit the scope of this book to it.

We have the power to liberate ourselves from the imprisonment brought about by our negative thoughts and destructive belief systems. Once we understand the power of our mind abundance will flow into our lives. The forces of nature show us that growth occurs in the direction of the light. If you take a plant, for instance, put it in a dark room and let a narrow ray of light penetrate the room, the plant will grow toward it. *The Infinite Power Within* is meant to teach you how to leave the depths of bondage and move toward the light and ascend to freedom.

Chapter 1

What Are You Afraid Of?

Chapter 1

What Are You Afraid Of?

One of the greatest obstacles to true happiness, fulfillment, and personal and professional satisfaction is fear. If we were to dissect our problems we would more than likely find fear at the core. Fear is the root cause of all of our negativity and our lack of success. Our mortality and vulnerability as humans cause us to have certain insecurities and anxieties. Out of fear, we seek to create some sense of security by ensuring that we are surrounded by supportive people, and by pursuing financial stability and fulfillment. Ironically, the same fear driving us to work hard to achieve these goals also creeps in and makes us think that we might not be able to hold onto everything we have acquired.

In our lives, fear surfaces in four primary ways:

• Need. We fear not having what we need in order to feel secure and happy.

• Loss. We are scared that we may lose everything we have.

• Acceptance. We fear others won't approve of our choices.

• Change. We fear change.

We must all ask ourselves: are our decisions based on fear? If we go through life allowing fear to dictate our actions, just how much are we missing? When we were a tiny baby in our mothers' womb, our lives were safe. In that environment, we were secure and comfortable. But were we really? Before we were born, we couldn't experience emotions, and we lived in a sterile environment. We were brought into a new world, full of uncertainties—but were also given the chance to feel love, excitement, and all of the opportunities our new world had to offer. I like to look at each day as a new beginning. I never know whom I'm going to meet or what new adventures lay ahead. Had I remained paralyzed by fear, I wouldn't have given myself the chance to live my purpose: to start my coaching business.

One of my favorite quotes is Franklin Roosevelt's, "We have nothing to fear but fear itself." I love this quote because it demonstrates that if left unchecked, our fears and anxieties can turn a manageable situation into a dangerous crisis. When we allow ourselves to be consumed with fear, we lose sight of all of the possibilities that life has to offer. I used to think that the fact that I was too afraid to do certain things meant something was wrong with me. As I've embarked upon my journey of personal growth, I realize now that it would be abnormal *not* to experience some forms of fear in both my personal and professional life. Fear is a natural part of life. Everyone deals with fear, and as long as we continue to expand our horizons and expose ourselves to new opportunities, we will continually experience some degree of fear.

It doesn't matter who you are: anyone and everyone, regardless of age or status, experiences fear during their life. Whether it is the fear of rejection, of not being loved, of not having enough or of being unsuccessful, the feeling is the same. True, some experience fear to a greater degree than others, but the defining factor for success and fulfillment is how we *deal* with our fears. Unfortunately, many people aren't willing, or don't know how, to change their fears, and will, over time, develop negative thoughts that impact their lives. Left unmanaged, fear, doubt and uncertainty may outwardly radiate.

Very often, we experience fear due to a lack of information or a lack of confidence. When we are ignorant on a matter, when we lack knowledge or awareness, our immediate reaction is to worry in the face of an unfamiliar circumstance or person. Worry and doubt can intensify into a feeling of fear, and later, anxiety. We can make a different choice and ascend to freedom rather than fall into a stream of fear.

It Starts With You

Many people prefer to stay stuck in their current situation rather than change. They desperately attempt to change the outside with quick-fix solutions without changing what is going on inside. They don't understand that their outer world is a reflection of their inner world. For instance, when a romantic relationship does not work out, many people attribute it to choosing the wrong partner. The next thing they know, they find themselves in the same unhealthy relationship pattern, this time with a new partner. They act similarly in other areas of life as well. People dissatisfied with their jobs will change jobs, people trying to lose weight will change diets, and people unhappy with their appearance will change wardrobes. The common thread is the perception that the cause of a problem is what is visible from the outside. People want to change everything *but* themselves.

Change has to start with *you*. Your first step is to increase your awareness by educating yourself. Knowledge, which is the opposite of ignorance, can be expanded through learning. When you understand something, you move away from fear and can build faith in yourself. When you have faith, you experience wellbeing. When you feel good, your body is in a state of acceleration. You can feel all the cells of your body vibrating at high speed and are at ease. You move toward the mindset of creating what you want, the ultimate place of being driven by purpose and achieving bliss.

My biggest fear was a fear of *people*. I was terrified of what others would think of me and how they would behave toward me. To avoid deception and rejection, I attempted to control others' image of me. I constantly measured their every word, every look and every move. I was seeking control over my external world, but I was far from being in control of my inner world.

In most of my relationships, I struggled constantly to reconcile how others perceived me with how I perceived myself. On the outside, I projected the image of a sociable, confident, strong and successful person. However, on the inside, I felt isolated, insecure, vulnerable, and unstable. I was living simultaneously in two conflicting worlds.

My relationship with a very dear friend, Rick, demonstrates my journey. Rick is one of the friends I consider closest to my heart, and I value his opinion in many respects. I have known him most of my life and I can honestly say that he knows me very well. He has been by my side during my highest highs as well as during my darkest moments. Rick is a very conservative, loyal, responsible and down-to-earth kind of guy. We always got along well because we have so many personality traits in common. However, since I decided to join LifeSuccess Consulting and to develop my coaching business, I began the process of a thorough self-transformation. Clearly, when undertaking a complete reconditioning of the mind, important changes start to take place. I no longer entertained the same thoughts. I felt and acted differently, all of which was aimed toward my personal betterment. While I was in the training program, I shared with my family and some of my closest friends the new venture I was embarking upon. I received nothing but encouragement and best wishes for success. Rick was my only close friend who did not know. I was delaying telling him on purpose because I knew that my new career path was not something he would easily digest. I waited four months before telling him because I was afraid of his reaction.

I finally decided it was time to tell Rick. I called him and offered to take him out to dinner for a very special celebration. There was only one thing that I asked of him, and that was to join me with an open mind. This was simply my way of preparing Rick for something out of the ordinary. Rick reacted with mixed emotions: he was pleased by my invitation, and intrigued by my secrecy. Even while a celebration is meant to honor good news, Rick was not one for surprises and enjoyed being caught off-guard even less. I figured Rick would be nervous for the rest of the week, even to the extent of losing sleep, in anticipation of our get-together.

Rick arrived at my place on Saturday afternoon, and I invited him in for a bit before we left for the restaurant. I immediately sensed by his non-verbal language that he was anxious. Wanting only to celebrate the wonderful changes I was experiencing, I felt awkward being around someone who didn't share my festive mood. I attempted to ease Rick into the conversation we would soon have by keeping our topics of discussion very light. My plan was to create a relaxing ambiance and reassure him that this would be an enjoyable encounter.

About an hour into the discussion, I sensed that Rick was getting a little impatient; he wanted me to get to the point. I explained to him that for the last few months, I had been seriously questioning my future in banking. I realized that I was falling out of love with the industry I had been in for the past fifteen years. I wanted to do more, be more and have more. I wanted to do what I really loved. Rick listened, but I noticed that his body was very tense, as if he was waiting for a bomb to drop any minute. So far, he had barely expressed any enthusiasm. I had yet to tell him the biggest bit of news, and already I felt that Rick was withdrawing from me. I continued to relate to him the comprehensive transformation I was going through and how motivated I felt about creating a new, more fulfilling life for myself, one in which I would exercise my true passion and excel beyond my wildest expectations.

I mentioned that I had started a training program a few months earlier and that I was planning on remaining employed until I'd completed the program. I told Rick that eventually, I would make the jump to pursue this new career path on a full-time basis and that it would inevitably lead me to quit my job. To reassure Rick, I insisted on the word "eventually." I told him that I had already come up with a business structure, a company name and a logo. In addition, I already had two-thousand business cards printed. Of course, I held off on giving him one right away. At that point, Rick was completely in his own world, closed down and very silent.

The more I talked, the greater the resistance I felt from him. I saw his body trembling with fear. Things were not going very well. Rick interrupted me and said: "Okay, where is this going, can we get to the point?" In my mind, I said, "I thought I had." I understood at that moment that I was talking to someone who was completely disconnected from the conversation. He was controlled by his fear of me moving away from him.

Rick never owned a business and was totally unfamiliar with the industry I was getting involved in. Therefore, I was giving him a double dose of facing the unknown. I reiterated to Rick some of my major points, hoping to give him a clearer understanding. In an effort at directness, I looked at Rick and said, "You are looking at a new businesswoman who has many interesting projects under development and who will be very successful in the next few years."

Rick looked at me and said, "Well, I still don't see what we have to celebrate." When I heard those words, I felt my body pressure drop, my stomach turn upside down and my newfound drive come to a halt. I took a few seconds to try to regain my composure. I now faced two options: either to let Rick's words destroy my ambitions or to stay strong and stick to my plans, regardless of his reaction. I chose the latter.

To ensure that our special plans would not be completely ruined, I suggested we leave for the restaurant immediately so that we wouldn't lose our reservation. I also thought a change in scenery might alter the mood. The rest of my so-called celebration was better than the beginning, but it was far from what I had envisioned our evening to be like. The next morning, we met again for brunch. Rick was still in digestion mode. He appeared preoccupied and deeply concerned. No congratulations were ever spoken and we parted ways after the meal.

As much as it hurt me to see Rick's attitude toward my new future, I had mentally prepared myself for such a reaction. I knew deep down that nothing he could say would ever make me change my mind. My decision was firm and final.

For the first time in my life, I was prepared to act on something without worrying about what he thought. I overcame my fear of his judgment, and refused to allow his skepticism to compromise the confidence I had built in myself and my budding enterprise. I felt such a burning desire to pursue this endeavor that I was able to withstand the strongest opposition, including Rick's.

This incident became a turning point in the relationships in my life. More and more, I now allow myself to be the real "me": the "me" I truly want to be as opposed to the "me" other people would like me to be.

Before my conversation with Rick, the stress of pursuing the approval and acceptance of others was limiting my future. Furthermore, this pursuit meant that I was not in full control of my life. I was dependent on someone else's reaction to judge the appropriateness of a decision I was making. In all types of social interactions, I tended to give others the power, letting them determine whether something was good for me or not.

I was continually torn between the need to please others and the frustration of compromising on my desires all the time. It was not uncommon for me to experience a headache and an upset stomach as a result of this internal battle. If we allow them to, fear, doubt and anxiety can stop us from broadening our horizons and expanding our lives. They can even make us sick. This book is a great example of how I refused to give into fear and limit my life.

I had never thought about writing a book before I attended a seminar in Florida. As the week progressed, I felt a calling to write a book. I had two choices: to let fear stifle this calling or to take the challenge head on and get my book out there. Fear didn't keep me from sharing my story and attempting to touch the lives of others, and it shouldn't prevent you from accomplishing your goals either.

Have you ever had a calling but were too scared to pursue it? Maybe you, too, want to write a book or perhaps speak in public. So what's holding you back? How many times have fear, doubt and anxiety kept you from taking advantage of all that life has to offer?

Far too often, we veer away from any type of new endeavor or "risk" because we're scared of something bad happening. Fear can prevent us from taking risks. The problem with this thought process, however, is that risks can many times bring great rewards.

When I was seventeen, I graduated from high school. Like all Canadians, I had to attend two years of college before moving on to university. At that point, I had completed all my schooling in French, my mother tongue. I had high ambitions for my professional life, and in order to maximize my career opportunities in the business world, I decided to pursue my college and university studies in English in order to master this universal language. The prospect of studying fulltime in another language was frightening, especially at this academic level. Even though one side of my family is primarily English-speaking and I had been exposed to English since early childhood, it would be quite a challenge to be immersed in a different environment. I was worried I wouldn't be able to get marks as high as those I had been accustomed to all of my student life. In the end, I graduated from college and university with distinction.

I am now fully functional in jobs that required a high degree of fluency in both languages, and am even writing a book in my second language! Many times, we focus too much on the fear of the unknown, and overlook the satisfaction and excitement that may occur as a result of risk-taking. In the space below, I encourage you to write down three goals you've been avoiding because of fear, and to describe that fear.

	Goal	Fear
1.		
2.		
3.		

I want to point out that like all fears in life, the ones you have written on your list are baseless. They are merely a perception of what can go wrong. Rather than attempting to unwillingly force your way past fear, why not explore the various methods that fear can be effectively released from your mind, emotions and body.

Some cutting edge research indicates that the mind and body are really one entity, not two separate parts. To try and explain this simply, it means that there is no separation or division between the mind, body, spirit and emotions and they each significantly affect the other. Studies recently conducted at Ohio State University and Tufts Medical School indicate that ongoing emotions of resentment and fear can actually suppress the immune system. An inhibited immune system is never good but for patients with other health risks, it can be serious. With this in mind, it is very important to understand that these emotions must be managed and you must be able to move yourself from a place of fear toward a place of peace.

So the next time you are scared or doubtful, remember that thinking to yourself "I'm going to fail" can actually trigger a physiological response. Living in fear can program your body to fail. When we know the right way to free ourselves from fear, we simply handle it as we would any challenge or obstacle, and then continue on with creating the best life possible.

In my experience, the best way to let go of fear is to understand that there are other perspectives out there— to break out of tunnel vision, and seek out new ways to elucidating the issue or situation at the source of my fear. Taking the time to examine your fear with a magnifying glass allows you to transcend it and remove the power it has over you. Only then can you see the priceless benefit at the end, much like when we say that after the storm, stillness returns.

The fear is the worst part of the storm and the stillness is the dissolution of the bondage that previously held you prisoner. Many of my stories in this book are testimonies of this truth. Removing fear from your life is the hardest work you will ever do. However, the rewards are beyond words.

Fact or Fiction?

As I continue to grow and learn, I am more able to distinguish between fact and fiction. In today's world, we are bombarded with myths ranging from, "you need a great education to make money" to "people who experience fear never become successful in business or life." One of the biggest myths I have encountered is that fear is a great motivator. I remember a few years ago realizing that I was working in the banking industry because I was too afraid to venture out into a new career. My position in the banking industry was lucrative, and I was good at what I did, but I wasn't happy. I stayed because I didn't want to risk any negative consequences, even though I knew it was absolutely essential to my mental health and wellbeing to deal with the situation. I was afraid of change, especially of failure, and I was afraid of what others might think.

After I attended a personal development seminar, I realized that I was making my decisions based on fear. This was a huge revelation for me. I had to sit back and ask myself, "Do I really want to live a life where fear of the new or fear of change keeps me stuck in a place I don't want to be?" After I asked myself that question, I experienced a myriad of emotions. Some feelings surfaced from childhood that stemmed from my need to seek approval from those closest to me.

As a child and even into adulthood, I had a deep seated need to be accepted by certain members of my family and friends. One person in particular kept coming to my mind: Rick. His opinion of me was vital to my self-esteem, which caused me a good deal of anxiety. To deal with this, I lived my life based on what I thought he wanted rather than what I wanted. If you've ever been in a similar situation, you know exactly how that way of living turns out. Initially, you receive the approval and acceptance of your peers, but as time passes, their expectations of you become too much to bear, and you falter and lose your authentic self in the process.

I allowed my need for approval to outweigh the consequences. There is a fundamental desire to feel loved, especially by those closest to you—but while I may have felt empowered momentarily, giving in to others' expectations took its toll over time. We can't live our lives based on what others want. Fear is a powerful force. In fact, it is one of our primary survival mechanisms. If we didn't experience any fear, we would touch a hot stove or get in the car with strangers.

Fear prevents us from getting into countless dangerous situations, but it also prevents us from achieving our goals. While fear keeps us safe, it should not be the primary factor in making decisions. If you are to live your life according to what is best for you, letting fear be the determinant of your choices can really hold you back.

Maybe you're like I was, and are afraid to change careers even though you are miserable. You may be thinking to yourself, "What if I can't find a job that makes me happy? I'm miserable, but I get a paycheck. What will my friends and family think? Will I have to hear 'I told you so?'" Maybe you are afraid to take a new job opportunity because perhaps the new job won't work out. But what if it does? A little trick I use that has changed the course of my life is what I like to call, the reverse question. In the past, I always thought to myself, "What if I fail?" Now I reverse that question and think to myself, "What if I succeed?" So the next time you are in a situation where fear takes over and causes you to question your abilities, try reversing the question.

Take a look at the results in your life right now. Are they what you want? Are you happy? Ask yourself if fear is your primary motivator in life. If it is, reverse the questions rattling around in your head and think about how good your life can be. In most cases, if you are making a good decision, you will learn that fear is natural, but it need not rule your life. Fear imprisons us, and except in cases of survival, it is rarely a healthy emotion to use as our primary motivator. Overcoming fear sets the course for a journey of great prosperity and success in both our personal and professional life.

Eliminating fear gives us the momentum to propel us toward our goals. Can you honestly say what scares you the most? If you truly want the life you dream of, now is the time to reflect on the fear, doubt and anxiety holding you back. Remember, being scared doesn't make you weak. We all have fears. The key is how we handle our fears and how long we dwell on them. Fear has to be conquered. Fear has to be faced. The first step to achieving the life you've always desired is to learn how to overcome fear. Understanding this important lesson opens every door to success and fulfillment. However, fear can be one of the most difficult areas of our lives to conquer because it starts in the mind. Often times, so many of us allow fear to take control over our thoughts and actions. In the remaining chapters, we will learn about the inner workings of the mind and how to tame our destructive thoughts and transform them into productive ones.

Anything loses its grip on you when you stop granting it power. This applies to people as well. Fear is an emotion, a state of mind. It is not real. In order to conquer your fears, you need to recognize what they are and what is causing them. Most people want to be, do and have what other people think they should be, do and have. Other people can represent family, friends, businesses, media, and institutions. Where do *you* fit in all this? It is time for you to control your fears rather than continue to let your fears control you, so that you can live the life of your dreams.

Chapter 1 Summary

What Are You Afraid Of?

• When we allow ourselves to be consumed with fear, we lose sight of all of the possibilities that life has to offer.

• Very often, we experience fear due to a lack of information or a lack of confidence.

• If we allow it to, fear, doubt and anxiety can stop us from broadening our horizons and expanding our life.

• In order to conquer our fears, we need to recognize what they are and what is causing them.

• Eliminating fear gives us the momentum to propel us toward our dreams!

Chapter 2

Who's In Control?

Chapter 2

Who's In Control?

Many of us feel as though we aren't in control of our own lives because we try to live our lives based on what others think is best for us. Living this way causes us to become frustrated and have frequent feelings of being overwhelmed and unqualified. This negative outlook makes it more difficult for us to find out what we truly want in life and to move forward toward achieving our goals. When we're in control of our own lives, we're able to eliminate fear and focus on our strengths and accomplishments, resulting in a life that is fulfilled.

I used to be very concerned about what other people thought of me. The opinions of my family were of particular importance. This was especially true during the early part of my life. Often I would act or behave in certain ways just to get the approval of those closest to me. I was acting out of some misguided sense of obligation, always pretending to be something or someone I was not.

I couldn't stand the thought of a family member or friend thinking badly of me or a choice I made. I would get very upset if I didn't meet their expectations. I tried very hard to be a good daughter or a good niece, and felt I deserved to be known as the "good and obedient" "child. The problem with that line of thinking was that I was so focused on what they wanted that I lost track of what I really wanted. It wasn't until I took an honest look at my life that I realized how much weight I gave to what other people thought of me.

Far too many people put their dreams on hold because they fear what other people think. Fear allows us to relinquish control of our lives, to grant external circumstances, people or events the power to determine our results. When we base our actions on fear, we become victims. Our lives are at the mercy of external factors, factors other than ourselves. But nothing should intervene in our happiness. When we are truly fulfilled, we don't give credence to any type of external stimuli or put stock in what others think of us.

I believe that each and every one of us needs to be in control over our own lives. We can't live according to what our parents, siblings or spouses think is best for us. Being in control of our lives means knowing exactly what we want and making sure that nothing stops us from accomplishing our goals. The benefit of being the captain of our own ship is that we get to decide what happens. We don't let others push their opinions and thoughts onto us. Releasing our fear and moving forward puts us in control of our own emotions and frees us to find our purpose.

Shift Your Focus

One of my favorite sayings in life is, "it is what it is." We can't change what has happened in the past and we have to accept our circumstances or situation and deal with them. For me, I knew that I had to face my fears head-on when I decided to make a life change. A few years ago, I decided to end my relationship of eight years with my boyfriend, who was also the father of my child. Since then, I have been able to reintegrate order and stability in my new life as a single mother with my son.

After two years of living in a small apartment, I knew I would need to have more space, both for my son to be able to play with friends and also for myself in the event that I decided to remake my life. The idea of buying my own home was becoming more and more predominant in my mind. Given my experience in banking, I knew exactly the criteria I needed to meet in order to qualify for a mortgage. I analyzed my budget many times, and concluded that even as the sole bread winner, I could meet the expenses of owning a home by following my budget very strictly.

I had always been reasonable in managing money and rarely overindulged in unnecessary expenditures. Therefore, I figured I had a good chance at finding a home that would serve our needs. In addition, as I was preparing a career transition and envisioning a considerable increase in my income in the near future, I became confident that I could find a suitable home for the moment, and eventually upgrade when my new business generated more cash flow.

As I started perusing the different real estate websites, I could not get over how significantly the price of single dwellings had risen in the past few years. If I increased my budget to meet the purchase price, I would be going beyond my financial capabilities. After a few weeks of searching and not finding anything I liked that was financially appealing, I began to lose enthusiasm. I kept playing all kinds of negative "what if" scenarios in my head, like: What if I don't find a house that I can afford? What if I find one and then I am short of money at the end of the month? What if my income is insufficient to pay for all of my son's and my expenses? What if the bank repossesses my home? I was reinforcing negative thinking and at the same time doubting my ability to accomplish this project.

The three major sources of stress are going through a separation or a divorce, changing jobs and moving. Already separated, I added on a career change and the possible purchase of a house. In other words, I would be going through all three at the same time! I had all the "logical" reasons in the world to be frightened. But still, I knew that if I succumbed to my fears, I would most probably give in and abandon my goals. I did not want to do that. To turn this situation around, something had to change.

The question was, which part? Should I let go of the idea of buying a home and wait a few more years? Should I downgrade my budget for the purchase price to create more manoeuvring room in my budget in case of financial trouble? Should I wait until I leave my job, and my business generates enough income to support my son and myself? Or, should I decide to look at this opportunity from another angle and give myself more options? I liked the feeling of the last question. When we stay paralyzed in our fears, we cannot distinguish the trees from the forest and our vision becomes blurred. We tend to panic and revert back to our safety zone. It is important to understand that there are always other options available. It is just of matter of tweaking our thinking patterns.

As I shifted my focus from limited to limitless, everything started to change. New ideas emerged. As I noticed more solutions and different ways of looking at this project, I felt better, stronger and more empowered. I took action in ways that produced the desired results, as opposed to unwanted results. For instance, rather than seeing this project narrowly, only considering buying a home as a sole owner, I opened my eyes to other scenarios, such as renting with the option to buy, buying with a co-owner, having a roommate to share expenses with or looking at income-generating properties. Exploring these ideas made it possible for me to widen my search and look at a larger selection of potential homes. Not only did I conduct research on my own, I also talked to friends and colleagues to encourage their cooperation in letting me know if they came across any interesting opportunities for me to look at. By giving myself more options and taking action every day to move in the direction of my goal, I gradually overcame my fear. I came to understand that my fear was coming from a feeling of limitation—my perception that an idea could be viable in only one way and pressing it to happen in that one way.

Our minds are blank slates. Whatever is programmed during your childhood sets the limits of what you ultimately achieve and the type of results that you get in your life. Some experience positive programming that allows them to accomplish anything they set their minds to, while others, like myself, grow up with what I like to call gloom-and-doom thinking, which makes them constantly look at the worst-case scenario, second-guess themselves, and seek others' approval. How many times have you caught yourself thinking, "I can't," "I don't deserve it," or "I wonder what they think I should do?" Remember that our thoughts, regardless of whether they are positive or negative, create our reality. So why not create a world of excitement and possibilities? In the space below, list some current situations or circumstances where you find yourself thinking, "I can't" or experiencing other negative thoughts. On the side, write some reasons why you *can*.

Negative thought based on a situation/ circumstance	Why I can

Why is it that so many of us dedicate our lives to the negativity surrounding us? Instead of focusing on what others tell us we can't do, why don't we concentrate our energy on what we believe we can do? Positive and happy thoughts allow us to construct an attitude where anything is possible. With a positive emotional state, we eliminate fear and concern. When we spend our days living in fear and anxiety, we are not productive. We are worried, most likely, because we are falsely placing value on the external factors in our life, such as information received from the media, governments, friends and relatives.

The key is to open yourself to different possibilities. When you do, you can see them right in front of you. Fear does not really exist. It is a construction of the mind based on misconceptions of people and circumstances in our current environment. It is when you narrow your vision and stay inactive that fear takes control over you and your life. By opening yourself up to multiple perspectives and by remaining in constant action, you don't allow fear to prevail. How our lives turn out depends on one thing: us. We get to choose how our lives unfold. Until we make the decision to release fear and take control of our own destiny, we can never truly be happy.

Detach

When we live with a naysayer, one of the best survival strategies is to detach, preferably with love. When I detach with love, I can still care for the other person but not compromise my sanity, health, finances or future. If we live with the constant critique of people who squash our dreams every chance they get, we'll almost certainly find ourselves worrying about what they're going to say, what they're going to think and what the consequences of their comments will be. Almost inevitably, we become caught up in their destructive behavior, finding ourselves trying to second-guess their thoughts.

If we allow them to, our critics will suck us into their world, and our lives will be dictated by *their* behavior and thoughts. Increasingly, we will find ourselves trying to control our world by seeking assurance and approval from that person. This was certainly the case with me and my friend Rick. Since my enrollment in the LifeSuccess training program, my life changed significantly. I became progressively more aware of my thought processes, good and bad, and how they influenced the course of my life.

We choose our thoughts, our thoughts control our emotions, our emotions influence our actions and our actions produce results. Therefore, when you change your thoughts, you change your life. This is exactly what happened in my life. Compared to the decisions I had been making throughout my life, my recent decisions are certainly out of character. I am no longer the risk-averse financial advisor following the rules and thinking inside the box. I am blossoming into a business woman who is developing an appetite for risk, learning to dare and to set highly challenging goals. Stepping outside of my habitual realm of logical and rational decision-making is totally invigorating, even while simultaneously destabilizing. I want to continue moving in this direction because it means I am growing beyond my comfort zone. When we let fear control us and be the basis of our decisions, it is as if we want to avoid making a mistake. There are no guarantees in life that we will always make the right decisions. Mistakes are part of our personal growth process, and depending on how we choose to look at them, they can be important events in allowing us to take a better action path.

Immediately following my decision to change and to attend the LifeSuccess seminar, life had become a real elevator ride, one that went only in one direction: up. However, upon my return from my training summit in Florida, I experienced an abrupt fall. My friend Rick was to pick me up at the airport. I was so excited to share all the good news about my life-altering week. Attending a convention like this one was such an intense experience. I was on an all-time high. I literally felt on the top of the world. I had so much to say that I did not know where to begin. As we drove, I started to relate everything that had happened, while trying to make him feel every moment as if he had been there with me. On the ride home from the airport, I continued to express my gratitude and enthusiasm about all that had taken place and the high-quality people I had met. There had been participants from all over the world, and the gathering of like-minded individuals had given everyone the opportunity to form life-long friendships and business partnerships.

After we arrived at a restaurant for lunch, Rick was eager to find out more about how legitimate and viable this new career venture really was. I understood from his questions that he was still very much concerned about my decision and the uncertainty of my future with LifeSuccess Consulting. Some of his questions were: "What are the statistics of people succeeding in this business versus the ones who fail?" "How long does it take to run a financially prosperous business like this?" "Are there people who do this on a part-time basis to make sure that their business is up and running before they leave their secure job?" In his mind, becoming a LifeSuccess Consultant on a permanent basis was a transition I was still pondering, and that I could reconsider this decision if I wanted to. I had already made it very clear to him in the past that my decision was final, but Rick was actually seeing this situation as if he was going through it himself, and it scared him.

As much as I was still living on the high from the past week and relating all the wonderful stories that happened, I felt a great deal of distance between Rick and myself. Needless to say, we were not on the same wavelength. I was stunned by how serious and calculated his questions were. In the beginning, I answered them lightly, not wanting to spoil my good mood. But, as Rick pursued with more questions of the same nature, I felt myself being pulled down with him, into the lowest frequencies of worry, doubt and fear. Rick is the type of person who avoids the unknown. Whenever he has a decision to make, he ensures that he has all the angles covered. Everything is carefully thought out should things not go according to plan.

I did not provide immediate answers to his questions, not because they were difficult or because I did not know the answer. I was unable to respond because all I could feel was his fear and I did not know how to break through it.

It hit me so strongly that I felt like a soft drink can being crushed in a recycling machine. Nothing positive arose out of this discussion. Rick did not express any interest in wanting to know how I felt or what I had experienced. All he cared about was my future security, and in his opinion, that meant keeping my current job until retirement. Unfortunately, Rick had developed the habit of paying more attention to the negative side of a situation rather than the positive aspects. And in my case, he saw more pitfalls than potential for success.

So, I burst into tears at the table. I stopped eating my meal because I could no longer eat, swallow and digest my food. "All I am doing is asking simple questions," Rick said. "I can't even get a simple answer and you have to play the emotional card on me. Anybody could ask you these questions." I replied that to me, he was not just anybody. He was a very dear and close friend. We were definitely not on the same wavelength and I did not know how to get through to him. I felt the atmosphere becoming heavy and gloomy.

I left the table to go to the restroom. I cried, became angry at him, and also at myself for allowing him to put me in that state. I came so close to leaving the restaurant without saying goodbye. I desperately tried to regain my composure and I kept repeating to myself, "send him love, send him love, send him love." As I stood in my bathroom stall, I looked at the ceiling and whispered, "God, please help me. I have to go back to the table and I don't know how I can find the strength to do it." I stayed in there a few minutes longer and I walked back to the table, completely at a loss as to what would happen next, but holding on to the little hope I had left and trusting that somehow my prayer would be answered.

I sat down at the table and Rick opened up the discussion again. I had difficulty putting two words together, and at that point, I was exhausted. I just wanted to go home. I looked him in the eyes and said, "Please understand that your thoughts are not my thoughts, your vision is not my vision. I can take full responsibility for my emotional reaction. But we are two adults here, so you also have to take your ownership of what belongs to you. You have to have confidence in what I am doing. When you do, it will completely change your mood and then, it will be my pleasure to address any questions you may have."

As we left the restaurant, we both felt good about the way this conversation ended. While driving, I looked up to the sky and said, "God, please help me. I don't want to stay in this low frequency of worry, doubt and fear. I want to go back to feelings of harmony, inner peace and bliss." After a few minutes it suddenly dawned on me that the incident at the restaurant was one of the many variations of fear that I had to experience firsthand in order to be able to enrich lives in the future, whether mine or my readers'. The incident illustrates so well how destructive fear is, and how hard it can be sometimes to look for the light when all you see is darkness.

As all relationships are mirrors reflecting back who we are, I could tell that Rick was lost in dark thoughts as much as I was. When we were at the restaurant, I could see that he was shaking when I was talking to him. This is not the first time since I had made the decision to start a new career that I noticed this reaction in him. Rick witnessed that I was talking a talk and walking a walk different from anything he had seen in me before.

He could no longer exercise control over me or influence the direction of my decisions like he used to. This was all happening at the unconscious level: I knew that Rick had my best interest at heart and meant no harm. It was all about emotions.

Fear is an emotion and in many cases, it stems from ignorance. Someone cannot be blamed for not knowing. Rick does not know, let alone understand, what I am venturing into, therefore his immediate reaction is fear—fear of the unknown. Rick lives at the mercy of fear and external circumstances. I could have easily let him pass on his fear to me, but I chose not to. I can only be responsible for my thoughts, not the thoughts of others.

When we have a negative influence in our life who invokes fear and doubt, we need to give ourselves emotional and sometimes physical time away from that person. To stop worrying or thinking about something is very difficult. I know that was the case for me with Rick.

Many of us find this challenging because no matter how hard we try, we can't just turn off our minds. But instead of worrying and being scared, why don't we try to do something different, such as taking the time to discover our true selves. Often, people who live based on the fear of what others think have lost their own identity because they've tried so hard to live up to misguided and preconceived notions.

Every time you replay one of those negative comments in your mind, reverse it. For example, if you constantly remember someone telling you that you can't, tell that little voice to shut up, and respond, "I can!" Rediscover the things that used to interest you, and maybe still do, and find new things to stretch yourself and help you grow as a person. We need to stop worrying about what others think, focusing on them and their needs. We need to grow into our own lives. This is what detaching is all about.

Dare to Dream

If we aren't in control of our own lives, we probably don't dare to dream. Why? It is simple. Because we are living someone else's dream. By this I mean we're trying to live up to expectations set by a friend or loved one. Some people dare to dream about what they want but they still doubt that their dreams will come true because of what they've been told. Before we can change our circumstances, it is important that our dreams are based on a strong desire, and that we are ready to let go of the fear standing in the way of achieving them. We must let go and forgive all past negative experiences and negative words other people have said to us. Nobody stops us from achieving our dreams apart from ourselves. When we live in fear, we are paralyzed. We do not believe in our own ability; instead, we look to external factors for advice.

We are searching for answers in the wrong places. We should be seeking guidance within. After all, only we can determine what is best for ourselves.

Once we release our fear and take control over our lives, we soon see that we deserve all the good that life has to offer. With a fearless attitude, we will start to dream more bravely about all the things that we want. We can't let external factors control us. We are in the driver's seat. When we take full control of our lives and our decisions, we are the masters of our own destiny. To be in control, however, we have to let go of our fear of what others will think and accept responsibility for everything in our lives. By everything, I mean all of it: the good, the bad and the ugly. Whether it makes sense to you or not, you must take total responsibility because only you are accountable for your thoughts, feelings and actions. Move away from blaming people or circumstances as the causes preventing you from reaching your goals. Don't waste a single moment. Start now and take control of your life by freeing yourself from your fears.

Chapter 2 Summary

Who's In Control?

• To be in control of our destiny, we have to eliminate fear and focus on our strengths and accomplishments.

• Instead of focusing on what we can't do, we must concentrate on what we believe we can do.

• Once we shift our focus away from fear, we gain confidence and feel inspired.

• We choose our thoughts, our thoughts control our emotions, our emotions influence our actions and our actions produce our results.

• Nobody stops us from achieving our dreams apart from ourselves.

Chapter 3

Unlocking the Mysteries of the Majestic Mind

Chapter 3

Unlocking the Mysteries of the Majestic Mind

In the previous two chapters, we've discussed the importance of overcoming fear and remembering who is really in control of our lives. If you answered the questions to the exercises honestly, you more than likely found a few areas of your life that need to change. I know when I took the time to open my mind and evaluate my life truthfully, I noted several areas that needed improvement. I tended to approach my relationships, whether social, work or family related, in a defeatist manner, meaning that I foresaw a negative outcome as more probable than a positive one. For instance, when I had a difficult boss to deal with, I assumed that I was unqualified to meet their expectations. When I had a conflict with a friend, I concluded that I was wrong, and therefore often took all the blame. Another example was my "self-talk." I can honestly say that I could count the number of positive thoughts I entertained about myself on one hand. Most of the time, my line of thinking was destructive and disempowering. I asked myself questions like, "Do you really think you can do that?" or "Who do you think you are to be thinking or acting this way?"

Creating awareness is the first step. If we don't take action, nothing will ever happen. The question becomes, just how are we supposed to make real and lasting changes in our lives? The answer can be found in one simple word: the mind. Understanding how the mind works is paramount to overcoming fear and unlocking the door to all of our goals, dreams and ambitions. We can change our entire lives by learning how to change our thoughts. I used to believe that I was thinking all the time. I would even get tired sometimes of thinking too much. I had the tendency to analyze and over-analyze. To me, that was my way of making sense out of life: by applying due diligence and weighing the pros and the cons of every situation.

Our mind and thoughts allow us to create, imagine and dream a reality where everything is perfect and the world is right. The problem for most people, however, is that their dreams don't manifest into reality. Real and lasting change has to come from within. It has been said that a person can have up to 60,000 thoughts per day. How many of them can we say are actually productive thoughts, ones that are directed with clarity, precision and focus? I can honestly say that my thoughts were, for the most part, unproductive. From one day to the next, I entertained the same routine thoughts, with slight variations. I was easily influenced by the people and circumstances in my immediate environment. I reacted to situations and I did not feel that I was in control. I spent a lot of time thinking about things that I did not want, anticipating a negative outcome and fearing the worst-case scenario. As a result, I ended up recreating more of what I did not want and it made me angrier. In reality, I was not thinking at all. I replayed the same movie in my head over and over. Some of the actors or locations changed, but the underlying script was the same. I lived on habitual thinking, not new thinking. I felt caught in a vicious cycle that I did not know how to break.

When we fuel our dreams and imagination with a belief that anything is possible, we soon see our biggest accomplishments and desires come to fruition. On the other hand, when we focus on the impossible, we choose thoughts that are based on lack and scarcity, and we shatter our dreams. I was raised by parents who taught me the value of money; therefore at a very young age, I started a savings plan. Being skilled with numbers, I learned how to accumulate money easily and manage it efficiently. At the age of 19, I made my first contribution into a Registered Retirement Savings Plan and I have not stopped since. I respected my budget and spent wisely. Debt was not an issue for me. About ten years later, all of that changed. A little over a decade ago, I met a man who was younger than me by a few years and we fell in love. I was living in an apartment at the time, and a year later, we decided to buy our first house together. It was such an exciting period for both of us. Our relationship was strong and we were both envisioning a bright future together. We started to discuss having a family. Our first home was a little small, so we decided to look for a larger house. Shortly thereafter, we moved into our second house. We made a reasonable profit on the sale of our first home, and the price of the new one was much lower. We found ourselves with mortgage and tax payments that were considerably cheaper. Exposed to a new lifestyle, we indulged in some luxury items and also invested a large sum in renovations.

A few months after settling in, circumstances that we did not forecast occurred. My boyfriend suffered an on-the-job injury, and a few days later, our dog was hit by a truck and was severely injured. My boyfriend couldn't work for close to a year, and his disability insurance provided less income than his full salary. We wanted to save our dog, so we assumed the medical care required for his full recovery. These two events alone were the beginning of a financial slide which made us very vulnerable. After extensive physiotherapy treatments, my boyfriend was able to reintegrate back into the workforce. However, he could no longer perform the same job and had to look for another line of work. Since we lived in a rural area, the employment opportunities were mostly seasonal and paid hourly wages that barely allowed us to get by. On top of that, very few permanent positions were available, which meant that the employees were temporary, had no pension fund, no paid vacation, and no insurance benefits. To make ends meet, we had to dig into a line of credit and use some credit cards. Bills arrived, interest charges increased and tension grew in the household. I did not like where we were headed.

Financial stress took its toll on our relationship. I was not accustomed to managing so much debt. As the financial connoisseur, I was saddled with most of the responsibility to keep us from sinking into deeper financial crisis. As I focused on our increasing debt-burden and felt the anxiety of trying to eliminate it, things became worse. I attracted more debt because I thought about it all the time. It consumed my mind and I was constantly in a state of fear—fear of lacking money. I faced the daily headache of trying to figure out which expenses to cut down on, how to reduce our bills and how to gather a few dollars here and there to at least cover interest payments. More bad news came when my boyfriend's wages and hours were cut back. We had to ask our parents for help. Some stability returned, but it was short-lived, since other unfortunate incidents continually hit us.

One piece of good news came during the summer when I found out I was pregnant with our son. However, the prospect of bringing a child into a precarious financial situation increased the tension between us. We could not afford to buy all the amenities required to set up our unborn child's room. We were lucky to have a cousin in the family who lent us all the baby furniture we needed, and other family members and friends who generously provided many essentials. With all of the cost reduction I was forcing into our budget, I did not understand why our situation was not improving. I did not realize that my thoughts were the problem. I was reminded of something I had once overheard: "The problem is not the problem. It is your way of thinking about the problem that is the problem."

Debt is a very negative word, in the sense that when you think about it, you do not feel good. It carries a negative energy. You cannot reduce debt by thinking about debt. The focus must be on being financially free. Just by pronouncing these words, you feel a positive energy, a lightness of being.

You cannot feel fear in the presence of financial freedom, whereas you can feel fear when you think about debt. The words we speak and the thoughts we choose have a huge impact on how we feel. Our feelings determine the actions we take and the results that follow them.

Our future as a couple faced more than just financial challenges. We sold our property not simply to overcome our debt, but because I wanted a separation. There is a great lesson to be learned about the importance of being in control of our thoughts. When we are in control of a situation, we can respond to it. Responding implies to think and act in a calm state of mind. When we are not in control of a situation, we react to it.

Reacting is acting on impulse. There is no consideration given to thinking properly. Thinking is the highest function we are capable of. It is the feature that distinguishes us from the animal species. Using our thinking wisely requires a deeper awareness of how our mind operates.

Our mind is majestic, powerful and capable of giving us the key to the unlimited wealth, happiness and abundance, so much so that many of humanity's great thinkers have dedicated their lives to the study of the mind's potential. Each of us has only one mind, and the sooner we know how it works and what it looks like, the sooner we can move forward in our lives.

Since our minds have the power to unleash greatness, and so many people have dedicated their lives to unlocking its secrets, why then do so few people actually access their mind's true potential?

A Picture Is Worth a Thousand Words

Our ways of thinking have been passed down from generation to generation. Sadly, some of them are damaging and self-sabotaging. Thoughts such as, "I'm not good enough," or, "I'm a loser," have the potential to prevent us from accomplishing our goals. I was brought up to receive and accept certain thoughts as truth. For instance, I was raised to believe that success in life is measured by career achievements. Therefore, you have to work hard and earn a reputation. Physical appearances were also very important in my family. I grew up thinking that if people approved of my dress code, my weight and my financial status, I would satisfy the so-called "social standards." Isn't it time we get to choose our own thoughts, ones that serve us better? How do we change our thoughts?

People think in pictures. As a result, every word we read or hear we associate with an image, and project it on the screen of our mind. When we have a certain thought, we instantly visualize an image. For example, if I ask you to think about chicken parmesan, you'd think of a succulent piece of chicken covered with marinara sauce and cheese sitting in front of you on a plate. You wouldn't think of a chicken sitting in a hen house. When I think of my ideal life, I don't see a bunch of graphs and charts detailing how much money and satisfaction I have in life.

Instead I think of a beautiful home I share with my son and all of the wonderful vacations we can take together. What about you? What does your ideal life look like? I'd be willing to bet that the life of your dreams doesn't look like a dead-end job and a stack of overdue bills. In the space below, write down what your ideal life looks like and then find a picture representing what you want (it can be from a magazine, the internet, or anywhere) and glue it beside what you wrote.

My ideal life is...	Picture

When you think of the word "mind", what image do you see? For most people, there is no clear image, and this creates confusion. In 1934, Dr. Thurman Fleet realized that people were being treated for the symptoms of their problems and not the causes. He saw the need to create a holistic medicine. He came up with an image of the mind by developing the concept of the Stick Person to illustrate the root causes of people's problems.

There is a direct correlation between the thoughts we entertain in our minds and the results we get in our lives. First of all, many people think of their mind as their brain. This is not accurate. The mind is present in every cell of our body. The mind is the combination of the thoughts and feelings which move our body into action. Our actions determine our results in all areas of life: relationships, health, wealth and spiritual awareness. The following diagram is a replication of the Stick Person.

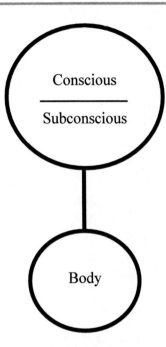

The Stick Person demonstrates that the mind is comprised of two distinct parts: the conscious and the subconscious.

The Conscious Mind

The conscious mind is our intellectual mind, our thinking mind. It is the place where our thoughts originate. Through it, we interpret stimuli through the physical senses: sight, smell, hearing, taste and touch.

The conscious mind has the ability to choose, accept or reject information. As you read this chapter, you can choose to accept or reject the information I am sharing with you. The conscious mind also stores our Intellectual Faculties, which are perception, will, reason, imagination, intuition and memory.

We are the only ones to choose our thoughts. No person or circumstance can make us choose what we think about. Our ideas or thoughts are our own. We become the products of our thoughts. So why, then, do the thoughts of our earliest influences become our own? We inherited a legacy of thoughts from our parents, teachers, clergy, coaches and other early mentors. They passed on to us their beliefs and ideas, many of which were meant to help us. Unfortunately, along with helpful messages, they also passed along the fears, false beliefs and prejudices that conditioned us to accept many limitations. Because these beliefs were transmitted at such an early age, and by people who loved and cared for us, it is difficult to question them, to free ourselves from the paradigms that limit us and interfere with our growth.

The Subconscious Mind

The subconscious mind is the brain's motor. It works all the time. No coffee breaks, lunch hours or sick leave. It's on the job twenty-four hours a day, seven days a week. Our subconscious mind is where our habits, belief systems and self-image are formed, based on early life conditioning. The subconscious mind is the emotional mind. It only has the ability to accept information. It cannot reject, nor can it differentiate between what is real and what is imagined. Since it has no ability to reject any idea or thought, it simply accepts every suggestion made to it. This is why it is incredibly powerful. Think of when you were an infant. Your conscious mind was not yet formed and your physical senses were still developing. You only had a subconscious mind in which thoughts, images and ideas were fed to you by your parents, grandparents and surrounding environment. At that time, you did not have the ability to process the information you received; therefore, you accepted whatever was transmitted to you. As you reached adult life, you found yourself with a multitude of thinking patterns, some of which were imposed upon you as a young child and others that you developed over time.

Our subconscious mind has no choice but to accept what we think. It has to accept the pictures we give it. The subconscious is also where our memories are stored. Our self-image consists of memories which represent out emotional connection to the past, but cannot help us in attempting to break limiting behaviors. The subconscious mind is the sum total of our past experiences and memories. What we think, feel or do forms the basis of our experience.

Any thought we consciously choose to impress upon the subconscious mind over and over again becomes fixed in this part of our personality. Have you ever had to give a presentation in front of a large audience or give a speech in front of your peers? You're standing on the side of the stage waiting to be announced. Just as you hear your name, you have a thought like, "I hope I don't trip," or, "I hope I don't stutter."

These thoughts are not uncommon, and happen to even the most seasoned presenters. We tend to engage in repetitive thoughts, especially regarding events or situations that make us feel vulnerable or uncomfortable. Our thoughts can become so repetitive that they interfere with our ability to function on a daily basis, causing anxiety, which in turn produces more repetitive thoughts. We can break this vicious cycle through awareness. We have a great deal of control over our thoughts once we are aware of them.

Until our repetitive thoughts cease, our results will continue to be the same. These repetitive thoughts take over and infect our mind. Our thoughts are massive and powerful and control our destiny. Our predominant thoughts must be focused on and in harmony with all the good in our lives, not on what we don't have or can't do. Make a conscious effort, and you will develop the ability to focus the power of thought on creating the life you desire.

The Body

The body is the shell for our thoughts and feelings, and is the instrument of the actions we take that give us results. If we don't take deliberate action, nothing will happen. Just as our thoughts are like seeds planted in a garden, the body is the fertile ground used to make them grow. Take the necessary actions, and tend to your seeds to make sure they grow. When I decided to improve my physical appearance, I knew that I had to make meaningful adjustments to create the lasting results that I wanted. I also knew that implementing changes halfway or putting in the occasional effort would not do the trick. So, I committed to a new regimen which meant that I had to change my habits completely: eat more balanced foods, drink more water and exercise regularly. Those are the actions I took. As I noticed the improvements on my body, I realized that with a thriving mindset, a healthy body ensues. Go back to the Stick Person diagram and notice how much larger the mind is than the body. Remember, the mind influences every aspect of the body, so take care of your mental self to ensure a healthy physical self.

By better understanding our mind, we can train ourselves to change the focus of our thoughts and actually see on the screen of our mind the good that we want. Whether we desire more money, better sales results or happier relationships, the process is the same. We must expect what we desire to come into our life, much like we can expect vegetables to grow from our garden after planting the seeds. The fact that the result that we want is not there yet does not mean that it is not coming. Not only must we feed the desire for the thing that we want, but we must also cultivate a positive expectation. If we maintain the desire, but expect a negative outcome to occur, we are being counterproductive, and are actually preventing the thing we want most from happening.

As an example, there were times in my single life when I was tired of not being involved in a romantically fulfilling relationship. I kept focusing on the absence of the man that I wanted and my limited opportunities to be introduced to new prospects. Even though I had the desire to find a healthy romantic relationship, I often expected the opposite outcome to occur, that I would meet a jerk, or fall for someone with a lot of emotional baggage. I was investing energy in what I did not want, and could be expected, so I stayed single even longer. When I decided to shift my thinking and start positively anticipating a qualified romantic partner coming into my life, I let myself feel the joy that his presence would bring. I felt excited about our imminent encounter and I radiated in a vibration of love.

As a result, I exuded a positive energy that led me to more possibilities to meet new people. Even if I did not know the details of when and how we would meet, I knew deep down that our meeting would inevitably occur. And it did. One of the reasons why I had such a strong faith is because I relied on my intellectual faculties, a concept we will discuss in the next section.

Intellectual Faculties

We often hear the expression that we only use 10% of our minds. Why? How can we tap into the other 90%? One way is to understand the concept of "Intellectual Faculties." Our area of expertise at LifeSuccess is the study of the mind and the marvelous powers that humans possess. We are all born with five senses: sight, taste, touch, hearing, and smell. By the age of five, the majority of children have grasped their ability to use their five senses to understand the world and the environment around them. The five senses are limited to telling us and showing us what already "is." They have no power to create or transform.

Intellectual skills, on the other hand, have the power to create and transform your habits. They are present in each one of us. Each skill identifies a powerful area of thought that we can use to change our habits and transform our lives. The six intellectual skills are:

1) Will

2) Imagination

3) Perception

4) Reasoning (both Deductive and Inductive)

5) Intuition

6) Memory

These skills are always at work, and in order for us to utilize our minds, we must exercise them, much like mental muscles. Your ability to have the life of your dreams starts with your decisions. The ability to make sound decisions is directly related to the development, integration and strength of these six faculties which, when exercised, expand infinitely. Let's take a closer look at each one of these six faculties.

Will

Will enables us to hold an image, idea or thought that we want in our conscious mind until it embeds itself into our subconscious. This allows it to manifest itself in our lives. The will allows us to take any subconscious idea that may have been present in our minds since childhood and change it. We do this by intense concentration over time and by repetition. Any habit that we want to stop or change encounters our will. The term "will power" has been used in conjunction with weight loss, addiction and exercise but it can also be used to stop habitual thoughts or negative self-doubt. My will has served me best in times where I was so focused on an idea that I was able to hold it in my mind despite all opposition, like in my stories with Rick. I was resolute.

Imagination

This is our creative power. Against all odds, great minds have created and invented everything from artificial hearts to the internet, thanks to the power of imagination, combined with the other intellectual skills. We imagine how we can do something or why we can't. When I created my company, I relied on my imagination. Ideas for my logo, slogan, colors and general business structure came easily. I was impressed with my creative powers, as I had never exploited my artistic talents before.

Perception

This creates meaning from events or experiences in our lives. We interpret these based on past events and programming. In relation to perception, everything is relative. Nothing has meaning, or is good or bad, until we think it so. Consequently, each person will have a different perception or interpretation of exactly the same event or object.

Never underestimate the role of perception in our daily lives. It has the power to alter our attitude and course of direction almost without our notice. It takes much strength of will to change perceptions we have held for a long time. Whenever I perceive a situation as disadvantageous, I talk to like-minded peers who may have a different perception of the situation, and sometimes, doing so makes me realize that my perception was incorrect.

Reasoning

Reasoning is our ability to understand the events in our world. Deductive reasoning is our default thought process that insures that we will continue to be a product of our environment. Deductive Reasoning relies on current understanding and conditioning at the subconscious level for guidance. When we reason deductively, we quickly reject anything that doesn't match our current understanding or paradigms. This guarantees that we will continue to act on ideas that keep that paradigm in place, and are likely to reject an idea that would move our life or wealth forward. We will also likely stay in our comfort zone when we are being deductive, and our attitudes will be created by our surrounding environment rather than creating the environment that surrounds us. We are purely deductive when our environment creates us, and we are being inductive when we create our own environment. Inductive reasoning, or "true thinking," occurs when we use our intuition, perception, will, imagination and memory to analyze new ideas, and then create and support the picture of what we want to see manifest with new thought patterns. I have often used deductive reasoning in the past when refusing to start my own business because it went against my beliefs of security and low risk. Now, I tend to use more inductive reasoning.

I walked out of my comfort zone and finally started my own business. I can visualize my success (imagination), I focus on developing business opportunities (will), and I follow my internal guidance system (intuition) with greater confidence when it comes to making important decisions.

Intuition

Often referred to as our "sixth sense," intuition is our ability to connect with another individual without even knowing or speaking to them. When we meet someone who immediately makes us feel good or positive, that person projects a positive energy and our intuition senses it.

When we meet someone who makes us feel negative or scared, our intuition immediately warns us of the negativity. Our intuition tunes us in, allowing us to see through all the noise of conversation and understand the essence of the people around us—who they are and what they are about. When I am with a friend or a family member, I can immediately sense their energy. When it is positive, I am automatically drawn to them. When it is negative, I feel a repelling force. Intuition is your higher being talking; it cannot deceive.

Memory

This is our ability to recall previous events and experiences. Many of us tend to remember only our failures, and those memories seem to linger much longer and be more intense than our memories of success. It is important to use our memory to bolster our confidence and self-esteem as we try something new. After all, at some point, everything was new to us—and yet we learned.

We must exercise our memory to work in our favor and remind us that we can do anything we set our mind to. Consciously focusing on past successes, no matter how small, improves our overall self confidence. Every person reading this book has succeeded at multiple things in life to get to this point. Claim those successes and remember them every time you set your course for a new journey in life.

Someone recently suggested I create a "me" file in which I collect evidence of past successes and triumphs. We often forget about compliments or special rewards that we receive. I have developed the habit of recording words of recognition from my clients, or tokens of appreciation from family and friends, in a journal to refresh my memory.

It is vital to take the time to invest in yourself and what's best for you. In today's hectic world, it can be overwhelming to discover yourself and rid your mind of negative beliefs, but let me assure you, there is nothing more beneficial that you can do for yourself. Think about the safety instructions on an airplane in case of an emergency: you must put your own oxygen mask on before you help a child. Otherwise, you will quickly pass out from the lack of oxygen and be more of a hindrance than help to assist your child.

We are each divine beings with infinite potential. You deserve to bring that potential to the surface. Invest in yourself and learn how to understand your mind and develop your intellectual faculties. You are worth it.

Chapter 3 Summary

Unlocking the Mysteries of the Majestic Mind

• We must exercise our mental muscles or mind just like we exercise our arm and leg muscles.

• Intellectual skills have the power to create and transform our habits.

• Our mind is capable of giving us the key to unlimited wealth, happiness and abundance.

• The conscious mind is where we originate thoughts and interpret stimuli through the five senses.

• The subconscious mind is where our habits, belief systems and self-image are formed based on early life conditioning.

Chapter 4

Harvest Your Thoughts

Chapter 4

Harvest Your Thoughts

Now that we realize how important it is to have a clear understanding of how our mind works and how our thoughts control our lives, let's put it all together and take the information a step further. In the previous chapter, I used a garden analogy and talked about how the seeds you plant grow and flourish with proper care. If a garden is ignored however, weeds can creep in and take over the garden, pushing out the plants you want. Our mind operates in the same manner. When we plant "thought seeds", it is imperative to tend to them and give them all of the encouragement they need to grow; otherwise, all of those negative thoughts will creep back in and suffocate the good thoughts.

The conscious mind is our *thinking* mind—where thoughts and ideas are generated—while the subconscious mind is our *feeling* or *emotional* mind—where we generate emotions. The body is where we see the results of our thoughts, feelings and interactions with the world around us. Impressing a thought upon the subconscious mind (which is present in every cell of our body) moves our body into action. The actions we are involved in determine our results. Therefore, to change our results, we must change our thoughts, feelings and actions. Only then will we get the results we want.

Every component of the "thought-feeling-action-result" sequence is important. We cannot just entertain a positive thought and hope for the result to manifest. Nor can we have the positive thought, become emotionally involved in it, and stop there.

As we become more aware of the undeniable truth behind the application of this sequence, we can learn to love ourselves deeper because we can think, feel and act freely without giving any kind of consideration or importance to the opinion or hearsay of others.

To create the results we really want, our whole being must be in sync. This means that our thoughts, feelings and actions are in harmony. We do not let any interference from the outside world come in. We are fully in control.

Our thoughts are extremely powerful. They are actually energy or vibrations, and emit waves like any other energy source. Thoughts can improve our lives or keep us imprisoned in a bad situation. We become what we think about.

What are your thoughts? What do you think about the most? Are your thoughts filled with possibilities, energy and prosperity, or are they filled with hardship, competition, lack and limitations?

So many of us spend our lives letting others control our emotions. People, however, aren't the only ones who control our emotions. People restrained by negative thoughts and feelings often resort to making excuses for themselves, blaming others, and other patterns of behavior that do not serve anyone in a growth process.

I know I have been guilty of this. I think back to when I would sit at home alone on a Friday or Saturday night, frustrated at having received no invitations from friends to go somewhere. I spent the night grumbling, pitying myself and blaming my friends for forgetting about me. Why did I come to the conclusion that my friends deliberately excluded me? Even worse, how sad that I ruined so many nights entertaining misconceptions and misguided feelings about the situation.

These negative thoughts and limiting beliefs are known as paradigms. In order to change our paradigms, we have to take action. To do this, we need to create a new set of behaviors and new habits in order to shift them and change our results! Once we put these into practice for thirty days, we will be amazed.

When we create new habits to replace our old paradigms and destructive behavior, the new good habits which support our growth become fun. They become an expected and enjoyable part of our day. If we skip a day, we find that we miss our new paradigms.

What are some of the limiting beliefs in your life? Maybe one of your limiting beliefs is regarding your potential.

Do you feel that where you are today is a reflection of your potential? Do you see limitations in your career potential, and that due to factors such as experience, skills, education, race or sex you cannot go any further? Just think about how limiting a thought like that is.

Where you are today is never a reflection of your potential. It is an indicator of your past thoughts and actions, including those harmful paradigms. As human beings, we have unlimited potential, and we owe it to ourselves and to those around us to get rid of restricting paradigms and use our gifts, talents and resources to create the lives we desire.

In order to form new habits, you have to reinforce them each morning and keep them every day. Habits are hard to acquire, but easy to live with. It is possible to shift a negative paradigm to a positive, life-affirming belief about your abilities and how your life will unfold. When you decide to change your paradigms, consider these important steps:

• Become aware of the paradigms you have.

• Change them to positive affirmations or remove them. An easy way to discover your desired new paradigm is to focus on the opposite of the current paradigm.

• Protect yourself from new destructive paradigms.

Take some time right now to consider what beliefs about yourself may be holding you back, and write them down in the space provided.

My three most limiting beliefs:
1.
2.
3.

By not addressing the power of our paradigms, we are setting ourselves up for an unhappy life. Paradigms determine our results, and only by addressing and changing them can we then change our results. We all have limiting beliefs about our capabilities. Some of them are inherited and some of them we acquired growing up. As a young teenager, I was often told by family members that it is important to be slim, and I felt pressure all the time to conform to this standard. When my body phased into womanhood, I developed a rounder figure. I was a bit chubby, without being overweight. I felt different than my friends and the models in fashion magazines because they were all much thinner than I was. In the external world, I realized that there was so much importance given to physical appearance. Your body was either an asset or an obstacle in terms of gaining social acceptance. On the inside, I came to hate my body because people were associating with my image as opposed to appreciating me for who I really was as a human being. As a result, I struggled for many years with my weight and low self-esteem issues.

When you address your paradigms, you may start with changing only one or two at a time. Therefore, it is important to start with the ones that are most harmful. Whatever the major issues facing you are, consider the ones most detrimental to you, the one producing the most stress. Challenge your paradigms and combat that little limiting voice in your head. The best way to do this is to tell it to be quiet and instantly replace the negative remark with a positive one. If, for instance, your little voice says "You can't do that," shut it down with an immediate retort: "I can do anything I want!" Remind that voice of who is in charge, and enjoy your new freedom from destructive thoughts and limiting beliefs.

Success Begins With Awareness

Thoughts become things and often our bad habits are a result of the way we think, including these "old lies" about our self and about the way the world or our lives appear to us at the moment. Humans are creatures of habits, and our habits form our future. We become accustomed to living with stress, fretting over life, continuously focusing on what we don't have or wish we had. The thoughts that usually accompany worry are negative and limiting, such as, "I'm not ever going to be successful," or, "I'll never lose the weight." These repetitive thoughts actually keep us from taking action and keep us in a vicious cycle of failure and fear.

Finding happiness and fulfillment is one of the most common goals for the majority of people in society today. Far too many people believe that this is important, yet are unaware of how their thoughts affect their daily life. Take a look at the list below and see if any of these comments sound familiar:

- I don't feel like I can do anything right.

- It takes too much time and work to be truly happy.

- I can't afford to have the life I really want.

- Nobody likes me.

- Good things happen to other people, not to me.

- I don't deserve this or that.

The thoughts we entertain, which come from a variety of sources and habits, control the way we feel. How we feel determines the actions we take, which in the end ultimately create our results. You might ask yourself: does this theory really hold true in my daily life? Without a doubt! Why, then, do so many people who want to be millionaires, improve their marriage, travel the globe, get the coveted promotion or live in a healthier body fail to achieve the desired result? The cause of all results, good or bad, resides within.

First, we must become more aware of the thoughts we think about. Awareness is the first step and enables us to direct our focus and get results. The more we grow in self awareness, the better we understand why we feel the way we do. This understanding gives us the opportunity and knowledge to change and create the life we want. Without knowing what is going on inside us, self-acceptance and change are virtually impossible.

With this knowledge, we can start to make conscious decisions based on what we want, rather than based on fear. If we don't actively make this decision, we'll stay in the same old habits as before and no change for the better can take place. Some of these habits are destructive and don't support our dreams. To help you understand this, let's take a look at the Seven Levels of Awareness below.

1. Animal: This is survival mode. Out of stress and fear, we react to our situation instead of respond. Whether we choose to react or to respond determines how successfully we move to the next level. Reacting is fight or flight and responding is stopping and thinking. Stop and think about how you are reacting next time. Is this the way you want others to see you? Is this how you want your children to emulate you? If not, change your response and move forward in life.

2. Mass: Here we are going along with the crowd and are controlled by habit. An example of someone who follows the masses is a person who goes along with everything they see and hear in the media. Masses are controlled by habit and by other people. These people are programmed to conform like herded animals. They fear what other people will think of them. To break from this habit, look for the ones who are going against the mass, and follow them. They're the ones who'll be successful, or at the very least fulfilled, where the mass will not be.

3. Aspiration: Terror Barrier: We become aware that something in us wants to live a richer life. As we break away, paradigms will try to keep us as before. We begin listening to ourselves and become stronger as individuals. We desire to be, do or have more. This level is desire without action. We are always meaning to do something, but we don't step outside our comfort zone—we cannot think or see how we can accomplish what we want. We worry about what others will think.

4. Individual: This level is combined with level 5. We discover our individual consciousness and begin to express our uniqueness as human beings. Through our understanding we begin to create or co-create with the Creative Master. At this level, we have begun to express our desire. To break away from this level to the next, we must use level 5, Discipline, because level 2, Mass is pulling us back.

5. Discipline: This is when we take the aspiration to move ahead, give ourselves a command and follow it. This is how we break away from the masses. We begin to express our own uniqueness as human beings, regardless of our situation or circumstances. We follow the commands which we have given ourselves.

6. Experience: We gain experience, which is what learning is all about. Learning is when we consciously entertain an idea, we get emotionally involved in it, we act upon it, and we change the end result. It's the change in result—the experience of the change in the result—that came about because we disciplined ourselves. We gave ourselves a command and followed it. We followed our aspiration to express our uniqueness. That's what the learning is. It is when we do this, when we step into this sixth area, and we keep experiencing greater things, that we move on to the seventh level and begin to master what we are doing.

7. Mastery: At this level, we stop letting the physical world control us. We begin to control ourselves. We begin to think and let our thoughts guide our world. This is freedom.

What level of awareness are you currently in? There are many books today that tell you about the importance of improving your life, yet they never really show you how. This chapter differs from those in that I'm going to teach you how to elevate your current state of awareness.

First and foremost, you must look at yourself and lifestyle with an open and honest approach. Don't judge yourself or your actions, just understand that if you aren't happy, you need to change the words you say and the thoughts you hold in your head. As long as you're willing to change your mindset and awareness level, you're going to grow and move forward in life. However, this is a lifelong commitment. Don't think that you can work on this on a Saturday and go back to work on Monday with an entirely new outlook. Long-term change doesn't happen overnight. This is something that you'll have to actively work on each day for the rest of your life. In the words of the famous motivational speaker Earl Nightingale, "Success is the progressive realization of a worthy goal or ideal." There is no better goal than taking control of our thoughts.

It's All About Perception

The good news is that we have the power to choose our thoughts. Often times, our thinking is on the wrong path, which explains why we do not get the desired results. In other words, we entertain negative and destructive thoughts. It is impossible to create a positive outcome when we think negatively. Think about it. How can a spouse contribute to creating a happier marriage when they focus solely on negative thoughts? We must love the thoughts we think about in order to improve any area of our lives. Then, we have to let ourselves be emotionally involved with those thoughts and act upon those feelings. This is where most people break down. They choose the better thought and they feel good about it, but they don't act upon their feelings because they are afraid of what other people will think, say or do. They remain immobilized. Or, they simply don't have a definite plan. They want to do something, but don't know what to do or where to start. Without taking appropriate action, how can we move closer to the realization of our goal?

Another common explanation for why people do not get what they want is because they focus on all the reasons why they can't get what they want. They have blocks, and are completely paralyzed by them. Blocks are really mental illusions that we keep reinforcing as we continue to focus on them. We must stop giving attention to what we do not want; doing so leaves us emotionally involved in a negative way, thereby perpetuating the same negative outcomes.

After my separation, I wanted nothing more than to start anew and create a different life. I was shattered inside and I knew there were important issues I needed to address. I wanted to regain my self-control and my self-esteem. Most of all, I wanted to live a balanced life emotionally, mentally and physically. I began this journey by reading a lot of books, most of them in the fields of spirituality and personal growth. These books were a catalyst in leading me to understand the power of our thinking mind and how it sculpts our lives. In other words, we are what we think about.

At work, I had the tendency to think negatively. I could even be very pessimistic at times. In banking, employees are evaluated twice a year: at mid-year and at year-end. In the beginning of every year, we are assigned specific sales objectives which we had to meet, and our bonus was based upon our final results. I was never a big fan of selling, and the performance appraisals were not moments that I positively anticipated. This was not because I was not doing my job well. I simply did not like the fact that, in the eyes of the employer, my sales results were the predominant measure of my worth as an employee. In my opinion, in a service-oriented industry, quality of service to the customer should be the priority upon which the company assesses its employees. In my banking life, I tended to receive performance reviews rating me as having "met expectations," which basically meant that overall, my sales targets were met from anywhere between 75% to 100%.

Through my readings, I became increasingly aware that my negative perception of the employee evaluation process was adversely affecting my performance review results. In other words, my final results were a direct reflection of what I thought I could achieve. I let my sales portray the value I thought I had in the eyes of the employer, and that boiled down to: not much. I decided to change that. I wanted to improve my results and feel better about myself, so I aimed for a performance review in which I would obtain the rating "exceeds expectations," which meant that on at least 40% of established objectives, results must significantly exceed expectations.

I started to pay more attention to my thoughts, investigating where they came from and why certain thoughts were recurring more often than others. I came to understand that I could choose to stop giving power to thoughts that were not serving me well, because they were not my thoughts in the first place. Now, it was time for me to exercise free will in choosing my own thoughts. I visualized the performance review I desired. I wrote it on paper. I fine-tuned it many times, really taking the time to feel the emotions associated with my new level of success and knowing with certainty that it would happen.

I could picture it very clearly on the screen of my mind: my boss entering my office, closing the door, sitting down in front of me, smiling with so much enthusiasm that she could barely hold it in and giving me one of the most exciting reviews she had ever had with any of her employees. Before even speaking one word, she would look at me with such pride in appreciation of the results I had achieved during the year.

I anticipated this moment with pleasure, joy and gratitude. I was building faith in my ability to influence the course of events and ultimately, be the creator of my life. As I changed my thinking mindset, my reality started to change as well. I felt more confident in front of the client, I presented the products and services more efficiently and I closed more sales. I monitored my results every week, and in a period of a few months, I could see a drastic improvement. This motivated me even more. I was experiencing the positive side of the Law of Cause and Effect; I witnessed the relationship between my thoughts and outcomes.

When the day of the performance review came, everything happened exactly as I had envisioned. My final results were impressive and I finished the year with sales that exceeded expectations. The scenario I played in my mind many times with my boss became a live motion picture. For the first time, I felt empowered and in control. I created the same result the following year.

To improve our lives, we have to be prepared to look at life from a slightly different perspective. Our thoughts are the single most important factor necessary to living a life of fulfillment. Remember, our thoughts actually control our emotions, which in turn affect our level of motivation and drive to stop destructive patterns. What we create stems from our thinking. Everything that exists due to invention does so because someone thought about it. We have the ability to choose. We can choose big, beautiful, prosperous thoughts, or we can choose small, angry, limiting thoughts.

It is impossible to outperform our own self image. So how in the world can a person take action to make their dreams come true if they don't first believe in themselves? Our paradigms cause us to feel, react and act the way we do towards ourselves and others. They are one of the main factors producing the results we get in our life, good or bad. Change is a part of living. In order to grow, you must also be willing to change. When you have a true paradigm shift, you operate with a new set of rules. You create a new way of thinking, being, working and growing.

Chapter 4 Summary

Harvest Your Thoughts

• We become what we think about.

• With awareness, we can start to make conscious decisions based on what we want rather than on fear.

• Repetitive thoughts based on negativity actually prevent us from taking action and hold us in a vicious cycle of failure and fear.

• It is important to nurture our thoughts with positive encouragement so that they grow and flourish.

• To change our results, we must change our thoughts, feelings and actions.

Chapter 5

Purpose: The Starting Point for All Achievements

Chapter 5

Purpose: The Starting Point for All Achievements

So many of us have spent the majority of our lives basing our actions on what others think, and as a result, paying attention to how we actually feel is a foreign concept for us. In order for us to find out what really makes us tick, we need to take a good honest look at how we feel. Once we've examined our inner wants and desires, we can get a glimpse of whom we are truly meant to be. Several years ago, I felt massively overwhelmed, and often thought, "Is this all there is to life? Is it ever going to get any better than this?" Many days, I sat and dwelled on this question. I didn't have any idea what I wanted because all I focused on was the question.

One day, after being instructed how to find my purpose, I actually sat down and took a deep, open, and honest look at my life. Very soon, I knew my purpose.

Since I started the LifeSuccess Consulting training program, I made the most amazing discovery, one that has given me wings to soar high. Not only have I uncovered a hidden treasure in myself, but also a clear direction as to where it will lead me. My life purpose was revealed. I believe that a life purpose is not something you find or make. It already lies within you. It may be dormant; it is just a matter of bringing it to your conscious awareness. Sometimes, a simple event or encounter can trigger its emergence. To me, a purpose is a lifelong mission and a reason for being on this earth. It is also an incentive to get out of bed every morning.

The primary reason I worked in banking and enjoyed it for so many years was that I was helping people reach their financial goals. For me, there was a thrill in making a difference in people's lives and allowing them to buy the home of their dreams, save for their children's education, plan for a trip or retire comfortably.

After a while, I realized that I had reached a plateau. As much as my contribution in the financial services industry brought me fulfillment and success, I did not feel that I was achieving the best of what I had to offer. My motivation was weakening, and especially in my final year in banking, I stopped taking on new challenges with vigor. Something new was brewing inside of me. I felt an intensifying calling to be at the service of people, and not just financially. Every day, I observed so many people lacking direction, purpose, self-esteem, confidence and so many other essential elements that lead to a happy, fulfilling and abundant life. I wanted to become a guiding light, a source of hope and change. Invariably, by enriching the lives of others, I would also enrich mine.

This discovery may appear simplistic or presumptuous to some people. For me, it created a unification between my heart and my soul. Both are now interlocked. This means that everything I do, from the simplest thought to the slightest word to the smallest action, is aimed at the betterment of my life and those around me. By becoming a better person and a more highly-fulfilled woman, I can have a greater impact on the lives of those I come in contact with. I see the reverse as also true. By letting others have a profound effect on my life, I also stand to gain from their presence.

Now that I have become aware that I want to help others, I have reached a point of no return. I am moving forward, neither looking back nor doubting my capabilities. I know with certainty that I possess the qualifications and gifts to help people grow and increase their level of happiness in all areas of their lives. I have been through many different challenging periods in my life and understand that finding your way in life is not always easy. Sometimes, we can feel discouraged or lost. When nothing seems to be turning around, sometimes we just want to give up. I am where I am today because I have invested time and money on my personal well-being. I have given myself tools to improve my life. By having helped myself, I believe that I am in a good position to assist others. I want to lead by example.

After interacting with clients, I can't help feeling passionate about the light I see glowing in their eyes. To me, light is life. Life is passion. Passion is excitement at its best, but in a calm and balanced way. Passion is in your gut and it never wanes. When your passion fuels your purpose, you can rest assured that you are on the path to fulfillment. Every day, I exercise my passion of lighting up people's lives through my purpose-driven involvement in their personal development.

Being a LifeSuccess Consultant has taken my sense of accomplishment to a whole new level. During our exchanges, whether one-on-one or in groups, my clients open up and share very privileged information with me. They provide me with an exclusive pass into the inside walls of their heart. They let me see the best in them as well as the most challenging aspects of their lives. Working as a facilitator in coaching and personal growth allows me to help these individuals discover and follow their inner callings. For some of them, it is the beginning of an amazing journey, while for others, it is a continuation. Regardless, I have the opportunity to embark on a life-changing adventure with these people, and I also get the chance to watch them evolve. I see important transformations blossom right in front of my eyes. I have the benefit of playing an instrumental role in guiding my clients toward enlightenment, and there is nothing more rewarding than that.

I have recently found another idea to express my passion: by combining my work with music. I played classical piano for many years. I love this instrument, and believe it produces the most sublime music. Before my coaching sessions and seminars, I want to play a piece of classical piano as a way to not only create an emotional bond with my clients and audiences, but also help them reconnect with their spiritual side. In a relaxed state, people are more receptive to new information and process it more efficiently.

When you operate at the spiritual level, you open yourself to possibilities and unlimited growth. There are no boundaries to what you can achieve.

Your Life's Master Plan

We can each have a life of genuine happiness. We just have to identify what we love to do, form a basic plan to create that end, and take the necessary steps to make it happen. A successful life is the springboard of two important items: purpose and vision. When we fall into an "Is this all there is?" feeling, we lack the spark that ignites us into action. People need a purpose. A truly fulfilling life begins when we push fear aside, find out what we want more than anything, and take action to accomplish it. It may not feel as stable and safe at first because it takes time and planning to learn how to make it all work, but when we have a purpose, nothing can stop us.

When my purpose became crystal clear, I was so excited. I felt like I wanted to help everybody! I started talking to family and friends about it, and building momentum to develop my business. Every day, my reason to get out of bed was to fulfill this purpose. It completely consumed my mind. My heart was no longer in the financial world. I was thinking more and more about living out my purpose full time; however, my business was still in an embryonic state, so it was not the time to leave my job. But I was not interested in my job anymore. I was torn between passion for my new purpose and the insecurity of leaving the bank. I called my personal coach for advice and he said two words to me: "calm confidence." In other words, he meant for me to stay emotionally neutral rather than swing from one extreme, excitement, to the other, depression. His suggestion was for me to make the best out of my time left at the bank while confidently building my business. He was right. Even when you shed light on your true purpose, it is important to pace yourself. This doesn't mean you have to slow down, but to calm down. Use this new positive energy that is growing stronger inside of you to win a long marathon as opposed to a quick race.

Nothing—neither fear, insecurity nor others' opinions—has the power to prevent us from living our destiny, unless we choose to give it that power. Before we take on any specific direction in life, we should determine what we want and where we want to go—in other words, devise a "life plan." By putting a definite plan in place, we eliminate a lot of the worrisome and doubtful thoughts which often curtail the achievement of our goals. We must first establish our purpose. Start by letting your imagination guide you and fall in love with a few ideas. Time is not a factor. The important thing is to provoke contemplation. After a while, you will lock onto one idea that will really drive you and lead to the establishment of a purpose. To express our purpose, we must build and maintain a vision. The vision will be the strategy to fulfill the purpose. In between, we have to set goals, which are a series of action steps required to accomplish our vision.

Think of this illustration. Our lives have a good deal in common with construction projects. Before a person can build a home or a high-rise building, they first have to have a blueprint. The same is true with our lives. We can't go after what we want if we don't have a solid plan. Can you imagine trying to build the home of your dreams (your vision) without a solid blueprint (your purpose)? Your goals will wind up jumbled: the kitchen may end up where you wanted your bedroom to be, and the den may not even get added. If we don't have a good schematic—purpose, vision and goals all together—of how we want our lives to be, they more than likely will look nothing like what we had envisioned. How can we build the life of our dreams if we don't have a master plan?

A word of caution, however. When formulating your master plan, do not let your goals be influenced by what other people think about you. I have some friends who think and behave in conservative ways. They say they are open to change, but when it comes to actually implementing it in their lives, they easily back out.

They justify this behavior by asking, "Why change something that works well?" As they see me undertake new projects, they ask me that same question: "Why change careers when everything is going so well for you?" A few years ago, I would have considered their thoughts and doubted mine. Now I respond, "Why not explore something that really appeals to me and can bring me greater success?" The opinions of those closest to you such as your parents, spouse, coworkers or friends don't matter.

You have the power within yourself to do what you want to do. Don't let the beliefs of others define who you are and prevent you from finding and following your purpose. Release fear, grab life by the reins and take control of who you are.

By defining your own purpose and vision, you thereby reduce the "knowing-doing" gap. Why is it that so many people know what to do to improve their results, but they don't do it? In many cases, it is because the fear is stronger than the desire. How can you reverse this trend?

When you consistently feed your desire so that it burns within you, signs of opposition and negative circumstances no longer stop you in your tracks. Your desire, or purpose, becomes your inner drive.

As I embarked on this personal transformation, several questions surfaced. I had begun asking myself questions like, "What does life really mean?" "What is most important to me?" "What have I been put here to do?" "What makes me get out of bed in the morning and live my life each day?" Purpose gives us meaning and confidence to know that we are living exactly as God intended. The word God here is not employed in a religious sense, but more so in a spiritual manner. I like to think of God as representing an unseen force, a higher power or a universal intelligence. We are divine creatures gifted with immeasurable talents and abilities. Many of you may think that your life lacks meaning. But, in truth, we all have value, and each one of us was put on this earth for a specific purpose. For some, their purpose may be small, and for others, it may be to accomplish great feats. Regardless of its relative weight, your purpose is important. No one was born to this earth by mistake.

Why are you here on this planet? What gifts have you been given that you can give back to the world? For some, understanding their purpose emerges relatively early in their lives, and for others, the answer comes quite a bit later. I know I didn't realize my calling until I was in my mid-thirties. People can't seem to find their purpose because they think it can be summed up in a couple of sentences. Let me assure you, your purpose is not something that is easily discovered over coffee or a weekend of introspection. It takes some deep soul searching. Whether the answer arrives quickly or takes months, we realize that we can only be happy when we are pursuing our purpose. Once we figure out why we are on this planet, we are not meant to state it in two or three sentences. It is important to take the time to look inside of ourselves and find that purpose.

Before you read any further, answer this one question. How would you spend your time if money was of no concern? Would you feed the poor, volunteer to teach children or paint? Whatever your answer is, that is what you are meant to do. Then you will be able to feel successful and happy with your lives as you live out your purpose. Each of us embodies our purpose in a different way. For instance, your desire to help save the environment may attract you to certain people or situations. Others may want to help children, which is why they spend a lot of their time volunteering at schools. For me, I knew I wanted to help people find their place in this world, which is why I decided to enter the coaching field. It doesn't matter what your purpose is. All that truly matters is that you explore your natural gifts and give yourself the freedom to let them flourish, which will invariably allow your purpose to manifest.

If you feel as though your life lacks purpose, meaning, or is just missing that certain "something," you need to listen to your inner voice, not your emotions. This self-development is so critical for us because, as we learned earlier, we become what we think about, so we have to be careful what we think, say and do. Even our emotions have an impact on our physical cells. They change and shape us into the people we are going to be. As we continue to develop and learn, we need to remember that there is nothing more influential than the thoughts in our heads. Stop for a moment and think about how happy your thoughts would be if each day you passionately engaged in something you loved.

You can find your purpose just like I did! I truly believe that if everyone in the world took the time to discover their purpose, release their fears, and do what they love, this world would be a wonderful place. There is a way for you to do what you love, and to do right where you are, wherever you are in your life right now. Below is an example of how I found my purpose. I took a real hard look at my life and answered these four questions:

1. **What do I want most in this world?** I want to help people find their personal best and live a truly fulfilling, successful and balanced life.

2. **What is the most beneficial way I can interact with others?** I interact with teaching, and coaching. I love to help people, especially when it comes to helping them live a happy and fulfilling life. I want to offer guidance and show them that if they stay where they are, that will be as far as they ever go. I love to teach about the power of the mind, and I use this knowledge to show people they don't have to feel "stuck" and can move to where they want to be.

3. **How is my true desire helping others?** My action increases awareness, open-mindedness and hope in people. I can lead them to forge an attitude that embraces positive and lasting change.

4. **What is the result of me living according to my true desire?** In embarking on a journey of self-discovery and profound transformation, people gain greater control over their lives. Consequently, achieving the results they want becomes a predictable outcome of their actions, as opposed to a reflection of sheer luck. They have understood and applied the power of their mind.

Using this exercise, I have defined my purpose as follows: I am passionate about taking people on an inspirational journey of self-discovery and self-empowerment. My role as a coach is to assist people in reaching a higher level of awareness of the power and operation of their minds, so that they can identify the real causes of the results of their actions, and become capable of successfully implementing positive and lasting change into their lives. I work in cooperation with my clients so that they come to realize that their results are a direct reflection of their thoughts, and that by delving deeper into their inner world, they can bring the limiting thoughts and belief patterns in need of adjustment to the surface. This drastic change in thinking improves their quality of life, and the outcomes they desire follow in a short period of time. Enduring happiness, health and wealth dominate their lives.

Take a moment and really think about what you love to do most in life. Once you have an idea, find your purpose by answering the following four questions.

1. What do I want most in this world?
2. What is the most beneficial way I can interact with others?
3. How is my true desire helping others?
4. What is the result of my living according to my true desires?

In answering these four questions, you will embark on some deep soul searching, after which you should be able to write down your personal purpose statement.

My purpose is...

Don't wait another moment to discover your purpose. Procrastinating only puts your life on hold. Every day you live without knowing your purpose is a day wasted. Finding and following your purpose gives you confidence and courage to go after your dreams. Through the journey of finding your purpose, you relinquish your fear and move into a new realm of thinking, where no one else's opinion matters except your own. True freedom is letting go of fear of specific outcomes and others' opinions, and living the life you were truly meant to live.

A Clear Vision

Finding our purpose is only the first step toward following our dreams. Without vision, our purpose is nothing more than a plan without action. Creating a vision is an important part of a purpose-driven life. Writing a vision statement allows us to dream, to imagine the life that we would like to have, and to determine the actions necessary to achieve it. In the previous section, you answered four questions that helped you formulate your personal purpose statement. (If you haven't completed the exercises, now is a good time to go back and do so!)

Your vision might be to own your own company, to create a new product that helps save lives, or to have a harmonious family and be the best parent possible. Again, just like your purpose, it doesn't matter how big or small your vision is.

You just need to have one. The first step to creating this shared vision is to visualize your perfect life.

Visualization is a powerful tool to help us live out our purpose. Visualization is nothing more than being able to see with our mind. Many people refer to visualization as imagination. There is a difference, however. Visualization requires us to concentrate intensely and truly believe the images we are visualizing. The concept behind visualization is using our power of thought, because what our mind sees and is made to believe becomes our reality. The more we visualize certain images, the clearer they become in our mind.

For instance, when I found my purpose, I formulated a clear intention of accomplishing it, even though I didn't have a clue as to how I would do so. I just held the vision firmly on the screen of my mind. One of the most important things to realize is that for visualization to work, we have to put as much emotion as possible into our vision and to use all of our senses, as well. When you visualize living out your purpose, you need to imagine not only how it looks, but also how it feels, sounds, smells and tastes.

It is transformational to have a clear and defined vision of how we're going to live out our purpose. There is a subconscious shift that occurs when we visualize our purpose. Our purpose is the destination and our vision is the GPS that helps us get to our destination. Our vision should be something that we can measure. Often, people have a difficult time thinking about their vision. The more they think, the more they get "stuck." Remember, finding your purpose won't happen overnight, and neither will discovering your vision. Take time and create a vision over several days if necessary. Just remember, you can't get to your destination without a map!

Find a quiet time when you will be free from distractions and visualize all of the possibilities for yourself and the steps that you can put into place that will help you achieve them.

Discovering your purpose and vision is vital to your journey. It allows you to connect to your true essence. Furthermore, it gives you a clear sense of direction, so that you know exactly where you are going at all times. When you live your life based on purpose and vision, you cannot navigate in fear for very long because you have established clarity and order in your life. In contrast, when you don't know what your purpose and vision are, you live your life amidst confusion and disorder, and this can easily open the door to fear. Life will continually bring its share of surprises and you will find yourself sometimes taking detours, but your purpose and vision will continue to provide the route keeping you on course.

Our lives are the direct result of the expression or absence of a purpose and vision. Of course, expression of purpose and vision is the ideal choice. The key to true happiness is to harmonize your purpose with what you specifically want in your life. What other people think is best for you is a reflection of them, not you. When you are aligned with your purpose and have a clear vision of how to fulfill it, you tend to move forward effortlessly in life. Situations, circumstances and events seem to present themselves to you. Friends, business associates or anyone else who can help you suddenly seem to be right in front of you. It is as if you are always in the best place possible to help fulfill your purpose. Life flows without any resistance, and you no longer feel as though you're moving against the current. Find your purpose and constantly feed it through a clearly-defined vision. Living with a purpose overrides fear.

Chapter 5 Summary

Purpose: The Starting Point for All Achievements

• Nothing has the power to prevent us from living our destiny.

• We need to explore our natural gifts and give ourselves the freedom to let them flourish.

• Our purpose is a lifelong mission and our reason for being on this earth.

• Creating a vision is an important part of a purpose-driven life.

• We can have a life of genuine happiness when we identify what we love to do, create a vision, and take the necessary steps to make it happen.

Chapter 6

What Do You Really Want?

Chapter 6

What Do You Really Want?

Once our purpose and vision are formulated, we can then begin to set goals in order to move forward in life and get what we want. A clear, strong purpose, combined with vision, goals and action is the fastest path to success. One of the best methods to assure your success is to set goals. Goals support our purpose and vision. Setting goals is a critical part of any successful individual's life.

When we sit down and really think about setting goals, it is common to set goals that are too general—for instance, that we want to become successful within the next year, or that we want to become entrepreneurs within five years.

But most of us don't take into account that the next year or five years are going to happen regardless of what we plan on doing. If our goals are not specific, we will find ourselves living the same life we live right now. If we want to change our future, we need to set specific and measureable goals. Being serious about our goals means taking responsibility to achieve them. Our goals should create a burning desire deep within us.

Transform Your Goals Into Reality

The commitment we make to accomplishing our goals plays an important role in whether or not we achieve them. If we don't decide to follow through no matter what, and then stick to that decision, we will never reach our destination. In order to achieve our goals, we must set ones that we truly want. Our goals should create feelings of happiness, fulfillment and confidence. The stronger the feelings, the more quickly our goals will manifest. If we don't truly desire something, it is easy to become distracted and fail to follow through.

One of the techniques I use to help me discover the goals that truly interest me is to make a list of all the things I want to have, do or be. Here are some of them. I want to have a prosperous coaching business and become an authority in the personal development industry. I want to have harmonious relationships. I want to develop multiple sources of income and substantially increase my net worth. I want to do more work with underprivileged children. I want to be self-employed and be in full control of my agenda, income, benefits and vacation plans. In the space below, write down all of what you want to be, do and have. Write down anything that comes to mind. Don't censor yourself with doubts such as, "I can't do that," or, "That's not possible." This is your life and these are your goals: the sky is the limit. We all have infinite potential and can achieve anything we imagine.

I want to be, do and have...

When your list is complete, read it over and find the one that really excites you. When I did this exercise, I learned that I wanted to teach people to reach their highest potential and live their life to the fullest by coaching them on how to take control of their thoughts and release their fears.

We need to visualize our goals. If we aren't able to see our goals, then there is a good chance that we won't be able to achieve them. For me, one of the best ways to see my goals is to write them down on a goal card. A goal card is nothing more than a small sheet of paper or an index card with your goals written on it. I carry my goal card with me everywhere I go and read it several times a day. As I review my goal card, I ask myself, "Have I committed to the actions I need to take to accomplish these goals?" and, "What actions do I need to do each day to move myself closer to achieving my goals?" By reviewing the goals we've written down, we create a constant image in our minds, making it easier to manifest them into reality. Below is an example of my goal card.

> By December 31st, I am so happy and grateful now that I am operating a prosperous coaching business. My main source of income comes from the services I provide as a LifeSuccess Consultant. In addition, I create multiple sources of income so that all combined my current annual income is equivalent to my monthly income.

Take a moment and review what you wrote in the previous exercise about what you want to be, do and have. In the space below, write your own goal card. Start by setting a completion date that will push you. Some people give themselves too long of a time frame to finish their goals. By giving yourself an extended deadline, you aren't motivating yourself to accomplish your goal.

> By _____20___, I am so happy and grateful that...

Now that you have your goal card, you need to brainstorm action steps you'll need to take to make your goals reality. Visualization will only get you so far. Thought without action doesn't equate success. With each step toward your goal, you will lose fear and gain the confidence that will help you move forward. I take action steps every day to fulfill the goals on my card. I am working with a web designer to build my personal website, where I will attach different revenue-makers such as affiliate programs, a membership login and a shopping cart. I am seriously thinking about adding an e-commerce feature to the site as well. I am also creating a plan to offer independent financial consultation services to preserve the expertise I have accumulated over the last fifteen years. I am constantly expanding my network of contacts and prospects in order to develop new business opportunities and earn the additional income I need to reach my goals.

One Step Forward and Two Steps Back

Why is it that some people set goals, only to find themselves living the exact same life in six months or a year? Because they've hit the Terror Barrier. What exactly is the Terror Barrier? It is the point at which we get so scared, we can't move forward or beyond our current circumstances. The Terror Barrier doesn't discriminate. It affects people of all ages. Sadly, some people live with the Terror Barrier every moment of every day. Once the Terror Barrier settles inside us, it tends to grow bigger each day like a tumor constantly feeding on our fears and insecurities. This is a natural process: as fear sets in, people stagnate and get more set in their ways. Have you ever driven on a dark road and then suddenly you see a dog standing in the gleam of your headlights? Even though you're speeding down the road directly at the terrified animal, it is frozen and can't seem to move. It is paralyzed with terror and cannot move from its spot, not even to avoid being hit and potentially killed. In much the same way, this happens to us: we get caught in our past and how we've always acted which causes us to become paralyzed in fear.

To move out of harm's way, we need to break free of the Terror Barrier. We have to find the old thoughts and beliefs that we're allowing to control us. All of these paradigms that control us form a strong wall that at times can seem unbreakable. For several years, I fought my own individual Terror Barriers and was able to break through these barriers. Even though I have been in banking for many years, I have had to perfect my sales skills because selling products and services has become one of the primary measures of performance upon which employees are evaluated. Selling implies approaching clients and proposing a product or service that meets a need or desire they have. For a long time, I was not comfortable in making that initiative on a regular basis. There were times I was so afraid of hearing "no" or receiving a bad reaction from the client that even as I approached them, I lacked complete confidence in myself. As a result, the client would decline my offer, and I felt even more terrible. I took it personally and let that affect my self-worth.

In order to avoid future rejection, I refrained from approaching clients, and inevitably, my sales results suffered. I remember discussions with previous employers who warned me: "Do something, otherwise your bonus will take a cut." I had difficulty accepting people saying "no" to me—not just in my line of work, but in my life in general. To me, every "no" meant "you are not good enough."

It took me a long time to understand that when people say "no" to me, it is not personal. It has to do with them. People say "no" for reasons that belong to them that I have no control over. Today, when I get a "no," I equate it with, "Thank you, but no thank you." This way, I remain emotionally uninvolved. How many paradigms do you surrender your power to and how can you move away from the Terror Barrier?

Awareness that a Terror Barrier truly exists and that you are affected by it every day is crucial to moving forward. This recognition is only the beginning. You have to step out of the Terror Barrier and into a new you. Breaking through the barrier begins with four steps:

1. Elevate your self esteem. If you don't believe you have anything of value to offer the people who surround you then you truly don't. You have to believe in yourself and your abilities. Stop listening and paying attention to any negative external factors. Regardless of what other people think, you have value to offer and your opinion matters.

2. Compliment yourself. Rather than tell yourself how bad you feel and how many mistakes you make, only allow your internal voice speak happy and encouraging words. Remove words such as "can't," "wrong," and any other words or phrases that invoke negative thoughts.

3. Accept responsibility. You have to accept responsibility for your fears and insecurities if you want to eliminate the Terror Barrier. You must also accept your mistakes or failures in order to overcome them.

4. Focus on the positive. When you entertain thoughts of fear, you are paralyzing yourself. Positive thoughts elevate your mood. When you think positively, you create the confidence to follow your dreams. Instead of uttering statements like, "That will never happen," focus on what you want to happen and say, "I can have anything I want!" Condition your mind to always view the positive components of challenges.

In performing these steps, you are taking control of your thoughts, bringing you closer to overcoming your Terror Barrier. Once you've mastered these four steps, you'll find that they apply to any situation or circumstance in your life. Stepping out of the Terror Barrier and stretching your reality gives you an entirely new perspective.

Obey the Laws

As children, we're taught to follow the rules and obey the law, or there will be consequences. We carry this belief with us into adulthood and make a conscious effort to obey the law and be good citizens. By doing so, we live a quality life free of trouble for the most part. What most people don't realize is that man's laws aren't the only ones we should obey. In nature, there are certain laws known as Universal Laws. These are the unwavering and unchanging principles that rule our entire Universe, and are the means by which our Universe continues to thrive and exist. How many people do you know that seem to have it all? You may be wondering what their secret is. I can tell you what it is without even meeting them. They understand the powerful effect of Universal Laws. They heed Universal Laws with the utmost seriousness, just as the majority of us obey man's laws.

In ignoring Universal Laws, we become caught up in trying to get more by doing more. If people would just consciously apply these laws, they would have more than they could ever imagine without doing half as much as before. These Universal Laws govern every aspect of existence and are responsible for determining our life experiences. They operate with precise, predictable and unwavering certainty and make no distinctions or judgments in how they operate or who they work for. They are at work 100% of the time, regardless of our awareness of or ignorance to them. Our conscious choice is the only thing that determines how they work and what they create. Once we start to align our actions and thoughts with them, we can begin to expect and experience outcomes which we used to think were impossible.

The Universal Laws include:

1. The Law of Gender. This law states that every seed has a gestation or incubation period. Ideas are spiritual seeds and will move into form or physical results. Remember that if it seems that you're not achieving your goals as quickly as you would like, that they will manifest at the perfect time.

2. The Law of Cause and Effect. This law states that whatever you send out into the Universe comes back. What goes around comes around. Don't worry about what you are going to get; instead just concentrate on what you're able to give.

3. The Law of Relativity. This law states that nothing is good or bad until you compare it to something else. Practice relating your situation to something worse and yours will always look good. If you practice relating your situation to something better, yours will always look worse.

4. The Law of Perpetual Transmutation. This law states that energy moves into physical form. The image you hold in your mind most often materializes in results in your life.

5. The Law of Polarity. This law states that everything has an opposite. For every up there's a down and for every

cold there's a hot. We tend to look for what is wrong. Focus on what is right. Always recognize the opposite, and then choose what you want to concentrate on.

6. The Law of Vibration. This law states that everything vibrates; nothing rests. Conscious awareness of vibration is feeling. Your thoughts, or paradigms, control your feelings, which puts you in a state of vibration. Pay attention to how you feel. When you feel bad, you put yourself in a bad vibration. When you feel good, you are in a good vibration. Think about all the good in your life and stay in a positive vibration.

7. The Law of Attraction. This law is a derivative of the Law of Vibration, which states that we attract whatever we are in vibrational harmony with. We do not attract what we want; rather, we attract what we are. What we are is dictated by the vibration we experience. Our emotions determine our vibration and our vibration is our ultimate point of attraction.

8. The Law of Rhythm. This law decrees that everything flows. The tide goes out, the tide goes in. Night follows day. There are days when we feel emotionally strong, other days when we feel emotionally drained. Free will takes precedence over everything. Focus on when you are on an upswing and give it more energy.

Once I aligned my thoughts and actions with the Universal Laws, my life changed dramatically. I had been shopping for a house for close to a year. I knew exactly the style I wanted, the size of the plot, the quality of the neighborhood and level of the privacy it offered and the price I wanted to pay. I visited several properties, but nothing came close to satisfying my criteria. It was frustrating that, particularly when I wanted something really adamantly and felt that I was at the optimal time in my life to receive it, it just wasn't happening. At one point, I found a house that I liked. It had many of the essential qualities on my shopping list, but it was not a perfect match. The construction style and the interior design was a fit. The size of the land was reasonable and the neighborhood was acceptable. But some of the rooms were small and the asking price was way above my budget. After doing some research and talking to some experts in real estate, I concluded that the property was overpriced.

As I was starting to feel a little impatient, I decided to compromise on some of the criteria that were important to me, and settle for less than what I was after. I made a low offer, hoping to convey to the vendor that there was a lot of room for negotiation. My real estate agent agreed with this strategy. When the vendor rejected my offer, I wasn't at all surprised. I wanted to test how far he was willing to bring his price down. The vendor made a counter offer, which I thought was still too high, so I refused it. This house had only been listed for a month, so the vendor probably wanted to wait for a buyer prepared to offer a better price. I was very disappointed. As a result, I put my house shopping project aside. There comes a time when you realize that forcing things to happen is not the best option to pursue.

As much as I was at peace with my decision, I needed to gain some insight as to why my house was not materializing before me. Perhaps my vision was not clear enough or my faith in finding the right house at the right time was not strong enough. Through constant study of Bob Proctor's materials and his core foundational principles, I was introduced to Universal Laws and how they affect our lives in very powerful ways. Not knowing about them is one thing, but being aware of them and not understanding how to make them work to your advantage is even worse. In the context of this specific situation, two of these Universal Laws were strongly at play.

For one, there was the Law of Gender. For example, we know that a baby takes nine months to develop into the mother's womb before it can be born into the physical world. It cannot complete its growth cycle in a shorter period. When an idea is not materializing within the time frame that we want, it does not mean that it is not a worthy or a feasible idea. It simply means that it is not the right time yet for its arrival. I kept that in mind. The second powerful Universal Law was the Law of Attraction. This law made me realize that as stubbornly as I wanted a house, I was acting as my own worst enemy and not attracting a house.

Because it was taking longer than I expected to find a house that really appealed to me, I was thinking about my current lack of my dream home. I felt more and more doubtful of finding the house I wanted and even perceived the delay as a sign that I was maybe getting involved in a transaction I shouldn't pursue. I entertained destructive thoughts, which were subsequently expressed in negative emotions. My emotions controlled the vibration I was in and attracted to me events in harmony with my state of mind. Therefore, I attracted what I did not want.

I became aware that I could exercise more control over my emotions by choosing my thoughts more carefully. As a result, I was able to realign my thinking so that I felt good about my thoughts, putting myself in a vibration that would attract what I really wanted. Recently, I wrote a goal card in April stating my aim to have amassed a certain amount of money by September. To earn this amount, I planned to provide quality and value to my clients through my coaching practice. I would use this money to buy the house I wanted, without any compromise, and leave my banking job sooner so that I could pursue the development of my coaching business.

A few months went by as I was keeping busy with other projects. One day, my intuition whispered, "Go on the real estate multi-listing website and check if there are any new listings." I immediately followed this cue, and as it turns out, I came across a listing which really caught my eye. The style of the house was exactly what I wanted. The pictures on the site were gorgeous, depicting an interior that corresponded precisely to my all preferences: a lot of woodwork, creating a very warm atmosphere; an imposing stone fireplace, now scarce in modern home design; open rooms on the main floor; and convenient bedroom sizes on the second floor. The plot was proportionate to the dimensions I was looking for, the main entrance was very private, and the backyard was large enough to function as a playground for my son and a cozy environment to entertain friends and family. There was plenty of room to add a spa, which was also an important element of my vision. Best of all, the asking price was much lower than my budget! I immediately called my real estate agent to tell him I was going to drive by the house to check it out after work. After work, I rushed to get there. I was completely enchanted by the exterior of the house and couldn't wait to see the inside. I asked my agent to request permission for a visit as soon as possible. He called me back to confirm that the first visit would be on the weekend! I was amazed—the visit fell on the same date as the target established on my goal card. The money that I had aimed for on the target date did not materialize, but I couldn't help thinking it was beautifully orchestrated that I got to visit the house on that date, which so far appeared to be the occasion I had been waiting for.

My agent and I arrived at the house on a Sunday. The seller, a retired woman, opened the door and greeted us warmly. As I took my first peak inside the house, I fell in love with it right away. I felt at home already. We ended our tour with the basement. There were no pictures of the basement, so I didn't know what to expect. It turned out that the basement was unfinished. On the one hand, this may have been an asset for the potential buyer; it meant I could convert the basement into a bachelor's apartment and rent it out to earn property income. Alternatively, I could renovate it into a finished basement for my own personal use. On the other hand, either project would involve considerable cost. Nevertheless, when my agent and I left, I was still interested in the house.

However, the completion of the basement represented an additional expense that I was not sure I could assume. We had a lengthy discussion calculating the cost involved and the return on investment I could expect in terms of added property value. That cost would be financed in my mortgage, which meant that my monthly payments would be higher than what I had budgeted. I was now facing a terror barrier. Should I go ahead with the purchase? Would it make me financially vulnerable? Would I be able to make ends meet? My agent explained to me that a house like this, priced as aggressively as it was, would be sold very quickly. His intention was not to put any pressure on me. Quite to the contrary, he was working in my favor and encouraging me to seize a great opportunity. What he did not consciously know was that he was forcing me to confront my paradigm—not being able to afford what I want—and tempting me to make a decision in conflict with this paradigm. I asked him to give me twenty-four hours to decide.

The next day, I called him and requested a second visit. Somehow, I felt that it was the right thing to do. This time, the vendor's agent greeted us at the door. For some reason, I introduced myself as Ms. Gannon, as opposed to Lorie, like I usually do. My agent and I walked around the house, this time paying more attention to important details and the overall soundness of the property's structure. A few minutes later, the vendor's agent approached me to verify if he had heard my last name correctly. Intrigued, I said yes, and asked him the purpose behind his question. He explained that several years prior, he had worked with a man that had the same family name. I asked him to give me his first name, and when he pronounced it, my heart stopped. He was talking about my father. What were the odds that the real estate agent of the property I was considering to buy would know my father? I couldn't believe the synchronicity.

After we left the house, I told my agent that I wanted to make a bid and we agreed to meet at my office the next day to sign the papers. While I waited for my agent in my office, I talked with a colleague about the house that I had visited the day before. I showed her the technical description and the pictures. She said that the house seemed very familiar to her. She asked me what the address was. I told her, and she replied, "I know that house! Is it possible that a lady by the name of Elizabeth lives there?" I was completely bewildered. I responded that she was exactly right. My colleague went on to explain that she knew the woman because her deceased husband had worked at our bank as a loan manager. I thought to myself, not only does the vendor's agent know my father, but now my colleague knows the owner of the house I want to buy, and her late husband used to work where I work. The coincidences surfacing in this story were absolutely incredible, and were instrumental in building my faith that this was really the house for me. How could I go wrong?

My agent and I met and we agreed on an amount for my initial offer. I told him about my recent conversation with the colleague who happened to know the vendor and her husband. I suggested to my agent that he should mention that I work at the same place her husband did, that I am a financial advisor with sound budget management skills who is already pre-approved for a mortgage. My agent agreed that this would definitely help turn things in my favor. After he presented our offer, he called to inform me that things went really well, and that the vendor appreciated to know some background information on the buyer. The following day, my agent called to say that the vendor had received another offer after mine. The vendor divulged her floor price, so the question became whether or not I was willing to raise my bid to meet her price. It was a small difference, so I agreed.

Several hours later, my agent called to give me the good news that my revised offer was accepted. I could not believe it. In the space of four days, everything was finished! There must have been great forces at work, because I later found out from my agent that the other couple's bid was higher than mine, but they imposed more conditions than I did. The vendor felt more comfortable accepting a lower price with fewer conditions. In addition, she apparently had a stronger preference for me given her familiarity with my colleagues and place of work.

This story proves that it pays off to know what you really want, because you can actually end up getting it. It also demonstrates that though we do not always control the order in which things or events occur, they materialize with divine timing. For example, though I am planning to exit the banking world in the near future, it was much easier for me to qualify for a mortgage while earning a fixed salary as a bank employee as opposed to being self-employed. Second, as I want to operate my coaching business from home, I have a perfect opportunity to convert the unfinished basement into a place of business.

Do not be afraid to set highly ambitious goals, ones that scare you as much as they excite you. The more you challenge yourself, the more you will find that the problem is not in setting goals that are too high and not achieving them. It is in setting them too low and achieving them. Know what you really want. That is something you can consciously decide. Then, work in harmony with the Universal Laws to help you achieve what you want. I fell upon this interesting quote one day: "Our job is to be skilled in dreaming, and the Universe's job is to be a master at scheming."

I hope that you learn to harmonize and align yourself with the Universal Laws, so that you can bring into your life that which you desire to experience. By discovering the importance of, and implementing, goal-setting; overcoming the Terror Barrier; and living by the Universal Laws, you will begin to release fear and rely more on your own feelings.

Chapter 6 Summary

What Do You Really Want

• Setting goals is a critical part of a successful life.

• In order to achieve our goals, they should be ones that we truly want.

• The beliefs that control us form the Terror Barrier, a strong wall that at times can seem unbreakable.

• In nature, there are certain laws known as Universal Laws. These Laws affect our lives in very powerful ways.

Chapter 7

Defy Your Comfort Zone

Chapter 7

Defy Your Comfort Zone

Let me begin this chapter with a question. What do most successful people have in common? Any guesses? Maybe you think it is money, drive or the ability to think outside of the box. Good suggestions, but unfortunately, they aren't correct. All truly successful people have the ability to move out of their comfort zone. Your comfort zone is a place where you feel safe and there is no risk. Now let me ask you another question. Is safety an illusion?

One thing we can all relate to is the notion of safety, which for most of us is what we perceive as the opposite of fear. When we feel safe, we are in our comfort zone. We believe that in regards to a specific thought, emotion or action, there is minimal risk. We feel quite sure of our position and we rarely second guess something we feel sure about. But, if you stop and think, what is risk? Is there not a risk in making choices that always feel safe? Is it not perilous to never question the bases of our thoughts and actions?

When I worked in banking, I managed the investment portfolios of wealthy clients, many of whom had very low tolerance for risk. They were not comfortable putting their financial assets at risk by investing in products such as mutual funds, corporate bonds and stocks, where capital was not guaranteed. Therefore, the allocation of their portfolio would be primarily in guaranteed investment certificates, where both capital and interest rate would be protected for the duration of the term chosen. However, I always cautioned my clients that by choosing safe investment vehicles, they were also taking a risk because they were limiting the growth of their capital and their investment return. Let's say that a client invested an amount of $10,000 for two years at an annual rate of 3%, and the interest rates happened to increase during that time. The money is locked in and the investor does not have the option of redeeming their capital. As a result, the investor loses on opportunities to earn a greater return. I like to compare investing in the financial markets with personal growth: the greater the risk, the greater the return.

We are conditioned to perceive risk as scary, even life threatening. We are very reluctant to explore the unknown or to welcome the illogical. We prefer to stick with what is familiar and comfortable. Our comfort zone is basically a melting pot of paradigms. Paradigms, as I have discussed in previous chapters, are a multitude of habits that are passed on to us since early childhood. Our paradigms control our perception and our logic. When we are comfortable, we remain bound and we stop growing.

If a plant doesn't grow, it dies. The same is true with us. If we are going to grow, we need to be able to take risks. There is no such thing as safety. The world may end tomorrow, and if we've remained in our comfort zone then we've missed out on a good deal of positive experiences. Defying our comfort zone allows us to face fear and achieve the goals we've always wanted but were too scared to go after. Staying in our comfort zone keeps us tied to our paradigms and prevents us from learning new skills. We can't set a goal greater than our paradigm until we believe in ourselves. We must be able to put ourselves into situations that are completely new. It is normal to feel a little bit of stress. But I firmly believe that when we are comfortable, we stop growing.

Conscious Decisions

Are you making conscious decisions? Are you manifesting the life you deserve or are you attracting what you don't want? Awareness is crucial to mastering conscious decisions to create your best life. Most of us are masters at unconscious decisions, which means that we make decisions based on habit. We do things automatically without engaging in conscious thought. Sadly, the things we don't want seem to predominate in our lives, and we unconsciously continue to draw more of them into our lives without understanding why. When what we have are the things we don't want, it is easy to focus on those things and situations. Many times we are unaware of our intentions. Our focus is reflected through what we think and feel. We are unconscious of how we are creating our lives.

I am learning to welcome fear as a sign that good things are happening in my life and that I am on the right path. I am thankful for feeling fear because it is helping me grow. In the recent months, I have taken many life-altering decisions and I am noticing that the bigger the decision, the greater the fear. One of these decisions is to quit my banking job by December 31st of this year. As I am writing these lines, we are less than two months away from the end of the year; therefore, I am relating this to you as I am living the impact of my decision. I am experiencing a myriad of emotions, ranging from exhilaration to panic; excitement to fear of failure; anticipation of greater fulfillment to fear of rejection; hope for prosperity to fear of financial collapse. I am completely outside my comfort zone. Like a circus acrobat, I feel suspended in thin air between two trapezes. Will I fall? Maybe. Will I grow? Absolutely. In the space below make a list of decisions you've been putting off because of fear.

I've been procrastinating...

It is important to understand that as you want to reach for higher goals, you have to think and do things differently. You cannot create new results with old habits. In the list you wrote above, take a look at some of the decisions you've been putting off and think about what habits have prevented you from making them. Your old habits keep you locked in your paradigms and you stay tuned to the same vibrational frequency. As a result, you continue to attract the same results. As I have made the decision to leave my job to focus solely on the development of my coaching business, I am highly committed to this goal and I already see myself having achieved it. True, it is not a current reality in my life at this point. However, believing it can be done and acting accordingly has led me to think on a higher thought frequency, which will invariably attract to me the people and resources necessary to support me in attaining my goal.

The day after I made my decision to quit my job, I called Tania, a very good friend, to share the news. I explained in detail to Tania the events that led me to this decision. I told her how I am juggling working a full-time job, raising my four year-old son as a single mother, seeing clients in individual and group coaching sessions and trying to meet the increasing demand for my services, getting ready to move into my new house in three weeks, and writing a book. I told her how I am running at full capacity right now, so I have to put the people interested in my coaching services on a waiting list because I do not have any more time that I can free up in my schedule. I explained I am at a point where my full-time job has become a hindrance in my business development. I felt that by being self-employed and temporarily living on a lower income, I would have more free time in my schedule to develop new business relationships and ultimately, increase my income. I expressed my mix of emotions to Tania. She could sense my high level of enthusiasm. She applauded my courageous decision and my strong will to focus on thoughts of success rather than failure. Tania believes that one who risks nothing gets nothing. As she recently lost her mother and received a considerable inheritance, she offered to help me financially should I need it. I had not intended to ask her for anything. Nevertheless, I thanked her for her support and indicated that we could reopen the discussion if and when the need arises. I believe that Tania appreciated how assertive, confident and determined I was about my decision, and as a result, felt inclined to provide assistance.

A week following this discussion, Tania and I went for supper in a nice restaurant. We were both happy to be spending time together. As December 31st was approaching and I was still standing by my decision, I felt it was a good time to ask more questions about the nature of her offer and the possibilities before us. As I mentioned earlier, I had never intended to ask Tania for help. I had some financial resources aside—not much, but enough to last me two months. But now that she had offered, I felt this was a privilege and an opportunity to make my leap more confidently without any financial worries. I asked Tania if it would be possible to advance $10,000 to my account in early January.

This would replace my salary for three months, which I believed was a long enough period to allow me to seal a few business opportunities and start earning some income. I explained to Tania that I was predicting a considerable tax return this year, given all the expenses I could write off in my tax report for the previous fiscal year. I expect to receive this return by May or June, at which time I would pay back her advance.

Tania responded that she wouldn't be able to loan me that sum of money in January, but that she would be able to offer it around March or April. At that moment, I realized that Tania and I had totally misunderstood each other when we had spoken on the phone. I thought Tania's offer was available at any time, whereas Tania, knowing I had some financial resources, thought I would only need her assistance come March or April.

After our conversation, I began questioning the viability of my entire plan. December 31st was only a few weeks away, and gradually, I began experiencing more anxiety, nervousness and stress. I was tired and I became increasingly overwhelmed with everything I had going on simultaneously. Sometimes, I had heat waves and even nausea. My mind was consumed by fear. I kept focusing on the risk of jeopardizing my financial situation and being short of money.

I perpetuated a mindset of lack and limitation. In terms of the Law of Attraction, I was not heading in the right direction. I knew that I had set a highly challenging goal for myself, but as a person who stands by her word, I wanted to prove to myself and others that I was accountable for my thoughts and actions. I wasn't really paying attention to the various alert signs my body was expressing. I kept pushing myself even harder, even at the expense of denying my own well-being.

A little while later, I became aware that the problem was not the goal itself, but the target date. Rather than trashing my goal and perceiving it as unreachable, I decided to change my plan, but keep the goal. As soon as that thought crossed my mind, I felt immediate relief. I re-evaluated my plan and decided to postpone my departure date until the following spring. I would keep my job a few months longer and could continue to develop my coaching business outside working hours. More importantly, I decided to shift the focus of my thoughts toward increasing my income, rather than being preoccupied with running out of money. I felt more and more at peace with this new date. My mind was calm again and my body returned to its normal state.

When you make a decision and you stand by your convictions, whatever you need to help you materialize your goals will manifest. The reverse is also true. When you begin to slide away from your convictions and fill your mind with doubt, you create precisely what it is that you don't want. That is exactly what happened as a result of my misinterpretation of Tania's offer. I let conditions and circumstances from the outside world control my thoughts. My mind became contaminated by fear to such an extent that I lost faith in my own beliefs, and as a result, I was unable to execute my initial plan successfully.

Keep in mind that it is okay to revisit your action plan even after you have made a decision. In fact, no action plan should be set in stone. You should review it periodically and make adjustments when necessary, while standing firm on your decision. This is where many people go wrong: rather than adjusting their plan, they either change their goal or abandon it. Remind yourself that things do not always go according to plan. However, this is not a valid reason to compromise on what you really want.

Tackle Your Fear

There often comes a time in our lives when we must make decisions —such as switching jobs, leaving a spouse or making an important purchase—that cause us to experience fear at varying degrees. Why is it that for certain decisions, we easily break through fear and stand our ground, while in other cases, we are paralyzed by fear and revert back to our comfort zone?

Fear is a destructive emotion and it puts our body in a terrible vibration. Depending on its intensity, the feeling can range from slight discomfort to panic. If we let it, fear can control our lives. Have you ever asked yourself what is the cause of fear, and how you can eliminate it? Fear originates from feelings of worry and doubt we experience when we are asked to make a decision that takes us outside our comfort zone. Our comfort zone is the security net home to the multitude of thinking habits, or paradigms, that we have been relying upon for so long. Sometimes a decision must be taken that creates an inner battle against our paradigms. Our paradigms scream "No!" and our inner being wants to say "Yes!" As a defense mechanism, we hold back because we are afraid and we feel like there is something to be lost.

When we keep entertaining the same thoughts and behavior patterns over and over again, we get used to a way of life that feels familiar and safe. There are no surprises, since we are not thinking, feeling or acting differently. We maintain the status quo. We perceive that there is no risk involved. We know exactly what to do, where to go and what result to expect. In reality, there is a huge risk in staying in our comfort zone because it doesn't provide learning experiences or personal growth.

Life tests us in many ways, and we can only go as far as our fears. To move beyond fear, we must open ourselves up to new ideas. This is not always easy. Let's look at what happens in our minds when we are presented with a new thought that disturbs a situation we have grown very familiar and comfortable with over time. At first, we may like the excitement of being confronted with a positive thought, or we may be repelled by the anxiety a negative thought brings. We decide to give the thought more consideration, but without getting too emotionally involved in it or acting upon it.

Our situation is not yet compromised and we still feel safe. As we give this new thought more energy, be it good or bad, we slowly become more comfortable with it. As a result, the way we feel about it begins to change, and we reach the next stage where we ask ourselves: What if I let myself become so emotionally involved with this new thought that it makes me change the way I do things and leads me to results I am unfamiliar with?

All of a sudden, the thought becomes frightening because it is leading us to unfamiliar territory. Right away, we question what the end result will be. We feel unsafe about doing things differently and taking risks. We worry about the possible consequences. We fear what other people might think or say about us. We experience anxiety because we automatically anticipate a bad outcome. We become mentally paralyzed. We are facing a Terror Barrier and we cannot contemplate the possibility of failure or rejection. So, rather than take the risk and grow, we opt for safety and revert back to our usual pattern.

In the past, I stayed in unhappy relationships for this very reason. I was terrified to initiate the break-up because I did not know how my partner would react, what my friends and family would think, and what repercussions this decision would have on my life in general. As opposed to breaking away from bondage and giving myself an opportunity for self-growth, I forced myself to endure a dysfunctional romantic partnership and hid behind the illusion of a safe refuge.

How can we break through the fear of making life-altering decisions? It is important to understand that if we want to overcome fear and create better results in our lives, we have to change our thinking. When we experience fear in the face of change, it is often because we focus on thoughts of chaos and we expect the worst-case scenario to occur. What if we did the reverse by focusing on thoughts of clarity and prosperity and expecting the best case scenario to materialize? Changing a deeply rooted habit takes commitment and discipline. To effectively integrate a change in thinking, we must use repetition. It is the first law of learning. Temporary or sporadic effort will not work.

With our conscious mind, we can choose new thoughts and ideas that serve us better. We impress these thoughts and ideas upon our subconscious mind by repeatedly becoming emotionally involved with them. This dictates the way we feel and pushes us to take action by creating new habits of success. As we become more aware of the control we exercise over this process, our confidence grows. We move faster in the direction of our goal and we produce the desired results.

There were times when my partner and I came to a mutual decision that it was in our best interest to terminate our union and have a chance at creating happiness with a more compatible partner. I chose a positive thought—the desire for a more fulfilling relationship—got emotionally involved with this thought, and envisioned myself living a happier life. I acted upon this feeling by discussing openly with my partner and working together with him to come to an amicable parting. As a result, both of us were able to move on in an atmosphere of peace, mutual respect and harmony.

There is nothing wrong in parting ways when we are in a relationship with someone who we know is not the partner best suited for us. It is not optimal to remain in a relationship for reasons that are fear driven, such as a desire to escape the truth or to avoid disappointing the spouse or hurting the children. We must not let fear be the decision maker in our lives. "Face the thing you fear and fear will leave you." As the quote suggests, we get rid of fear by facing it. Remember, any type of change involves risk. That means risking a wrong move, a bad decision, loss of some money or even a major setback. It also means that you must be adaptable to changing circumstances. Keep focused and remember that no matter how difficult times may seem, with a determined mindset and a responsible attitude, you will achieve your goals.

Goals that don't challenge us keep us in our current circumstances. If we want to move forward, we have to have the courage to stretch our abilities and defy our comfort zone. We need to release our fear, break out of our safety net, and force ourselves to learn new and difficult skills. We will never achieve great things without challenging ourselves. Stretch yourself and be serious about what you want to achieve.

Chapter 7 Summary

Defy Your Comfort Zone

• Our comfort zone is basically a melting pot of paradigms.

• We cannot create new results with old habits.

• Rather than taking a risk and growing, we opt for safety and revert back to our usual patterns.

• Life tests us in many ways and we can only go as far as our fears.

• We must not let fear be the decision maker in our lives.

Chapter 8

A Whole New World

Chapter 8

A Whole New World

There is a lantern burning in each and every one of you. For so long, the light in you has been dimmed. It is now time to reactivate the flame and stoke its fire so that you become completely illuminated. I believe that everybody walking on this earth should radiate in light. We can all be spirits in bloom and spend our days doing what we really love to do. In other words, we can all be completely purpose-driven. What a sublime picture.

My personal journey in increasing my knowledge and awareness has brought about some interesting surprises. For one, I have come to change the way I interact with people by becoming more open and compassionate toward other human beings. I have also come to learn anew the origin and definition of some words. I must say that I have grown fond of three words in particular that have considerably enriched my life and also helped lessen the intensity of my fears. These words are: humility, inspiration, and responsibility. As I apply them daily, my life continues to evolve on the path of promise and profound contentment. I now keep humility, inspiration, and responsibility in mind whenever I deal with a human being, and this takes our interaction to a whole new level.

Humility

Thus far, we've discussed the importance of taking control of our thoughts and releasing fear, since if we do so we will find success and happiness. What a shock, then, when so many people finally achieve the goals they have worked so hard for only to discover that the attainment of their goals didn't bring them the happiness they anticipated. Could the dissatisfaction be because our definition of success is faulty? Would we find true happiness in success if we moved from a self-centered, worldly view of success to one defined by humility?

Our goal is to find happiness and success, but some people who actually find it feel dissatisfied after the initial high has worn off. We can't proceed to the next level in life, one of true fulfillment and peace, until we let go of arrogance and preconceived notions. Humility is what brings the right balance into our lives. Instead of thinking that we are better than others, we recognize that each one of us has the same unlimited potential, and in turn, we grow more in the knowledge of who we truly are.

It is humility more than authority that inspires cooperation; therefore, humility is a fundamental characteristic of a successful person. A person's humility sometimes means the difference between going at something alone and waiting for help. Feelings of superiority over the people you serve or people you work with can lead to irresponsible decisions and unnecessary actions. In life, there is no place for superiority. Everyone is equal in this world, and arrogance or stubbornness can lead to hurt, feelings of unworthiness and fear.

Living in a culture that places such great value on power and money, we can at times find it difficult to view success with humility at its core. What humility will reveal to us, if we listen to our inner voice, is that true success is to love others, accept them for who they are, and not to judge them.

It can seem counterintuitive to believe that through humility, we can actually achieve greater success. Humility is somewhat difficult to learn and to define, but when we see it in someone else's life, we know it instantly. My mentor Bob Proctor said the following words of wisdom, which really resonated with me: "We can either love people or judge them, but we cannot do both at the same time." So, when we judge people, we don't love them for who they really are. We attach significance to their difference. The basis of our love for them becomes conditional. In contrast, when we love others unconditionally, we move beyond judgment. We are in a state of acceptance, as opposed to resistance, and that is where love expands. Loving others also means loving oneself.

Kevin Hall, an amazing person and author whom I met at the LifeSuccess training seminar, shared this interesting idea: "If you feel inferior to someone, you can also feel superior to another." Comparing ourselves to others, much like judging, can be an expression of fear: fear of displeasing people, not meeting their standards, or not living up to their expectations. If you find that despite your efforts to control every aspect of your life, you are not finding the happiness and peace you seek, the answer can be found in discovering humility. By opening your mind and becoming compassionate and nonjudgmental, you can reach heights of success you never imagined.

In my own life, I have used the richness of these insights to reacquaint myself with the meaning of the word "love". Whenever I am faced with people who do not agree with what I think or do, I keep these references in mind and grow a larger place in my heart to practice humility. For instance, I had supper with my friend Tania recently. We have a good and honest relationship. We do not see each other as often as we would like, but we speak on the phone regularly and can talk for hours. At the restaurant, amidst great conversations on a variety of subjects, I felt inclined to ask her the following: "Tania, since I have decided to invest significantly in my personal development by enrolling in the LifeSuccess training program and joining Bob Proctor's international team of consultants, have you found that I have changed?"

There was a moment of silence and I could see that Tania was mulling over her answer. Tania is a very delicate person and she is gifted in talking to a person in a way that does not hurt their feelings. Tania replied, "Well, yes, you have changed. I can see how motivated and excited you are about everything you are learning and applying in your life. However, when I talk to you about a difficult challenge I am going through, at times I sense that the feelings I am expressing are not important to you. In other words, you find my situation trivial and you think I should be able to overcome it very easily. It is as if you are going at one-hundred miles per hour whereas I am only going thirty. I want to catch up with you, but I feel like you are going too fast for me." I realized that some of the people I talk to or work with in my coaching business may also feel the same way. This incident was critical in teaching me a lesson in humility, and teaching me that we can learn from every experience and every person in life. We may not always like the way things unfold. The important thing is to take the lesson and move on.

Inspiration Via Intuition

Inspiration means "in spirit," to be in connection with a higher and divine order. Spirit is evenly present in all places at all times. We are spiritual beings gifted with an intellect and living in a physical body. This means that we can use the power of thought to form any idea and manifest it into our reality. To me, this is the pathway to unlimited inspiration because we open the gates of our marvelous mind and let energy flow from a higher frequency, our spirit, to a lower frequency, our physical body. Most people unconsciously operate in the opposite direction: in choosing their thoughts and building ideas, they follow their current results. Therefore, their physical reality, rather than their true spiritual nature, becomes the modus operandi for their way of life. We must not limit our goals and dreams to what we perceive through our physical senses only. The fact that something is not yet visible to the naked eye does not make it impossible. Everything originates from thought. We can use the power of thought to build an image on the screen of our mind and use our faculties of imagination and intuition to guide us on the path to materializing our goals. Through intuition, we receive thoughts, images and ideas. We become inspired by them, and then we can use our imagination to transform these thoughts, images and ideas into reality.

Learn to trust your feelings sometimes. Make guesses about people based on feeling (such as what they do for a living or what mood they are in) and then find out whether you're right. You will be surprised at how often you are. Practice relying on your intuition regularly and this will strengthen your intuitive powers. Remember, patterns are key.

Intuition is a quiet, powerful inner knowledge of truth. Intuition is your inner connection to a larger truth, and connection is your intuitive relationship to a bigger picture. When you are not feeling particularly connected, you will likely be easily distracted, unengaged and even bored with the event, conversation, or person you are involved with at the moment. When you are not accessing your intuition, you are likely to experience not only distraction and boredom, but also confusion, a sense of being overwhelmed by the monotony of your daily life. If you find yourself experiencing those sensations, and you want change, it's time to view your inner and outer connections.

The Universal Laws show us that the outer connections are really only a symptom of our inner connections. That is, our world is a reflection of what's happening inside us. Our satisfaction with our relationships, opportunities, finances, home, and other facets of life has a direct correlation with how we feel about them, focus on them, and how we work with our intuition in creating them.

The most important inner connection we can have is the one with ourselves through our intuition. Remember, intuition is a quiet inner voice; it won't shout to be heard, judge your choices, or stop your free will in acting in the physical world. Intuition is what is waiting to be listened to, and is always accessible to help you handle your world.

Intuition is instinctively knowing or perceiving something before you have all the facts. From business to mysticism, intuition plays a part in knowing when something just doesn't seem right or is out of sync. When people say that they "just knew" or could feel it in their gut, that is intuition speaking. Intuition is vibrational healing, subtle energies that are foreign to most people. Intuition is not an opinion or a rational kind of thinking. Intuition is when inside your head, you just know. You have a gut feeling that you should not continue doing whatever it is you are doing, or that you should choose another path, whether because something bad might happen, or because there is something you are unaware of. Inside your mind and in your heart, you know. It is a concept that is quite difficult to explain to people, especially when some prefer to think of you as an irrational thinker. Those people who know without knowing how they know, later realize that they followed their intuition. When should you follow your intuition? All the time. I have often followed my intuition and have rarely been misguided by it.

Most people are born with all these abilities. Everyone has an inner guide that works with them and communicates continuously with their soul. Some people actually see these beings. It may be crystal clear, as real as you and me, or it might be a very bright light, or ghostlike or shadowy. I'm sure there are as many ways to see them as there are people.

Accessing your intuition consists of tuning into and correctly interpreting the subtle vibrations of energy you receive. These energetic impulses may be invisible and intangible, yet they are real and we are all capable of accessing this information by paying attention and by learning how to tune in and interpret these subtle pulses of energy. Everything is energy. Energy is vibration. Everything that exists is giving off a vibration. All vibration creates sound, usually out of our hearing range. Some people can tap into that. Your guides and angels, nature spirits, and ascended masters are all present, right here right now. They just exist in dimensions that vibrate faster than ours. Most people can't see or hear or feel them because you have to raise your own vibration in order to tap into those dimensions.

This is how I use inspiration and intuition to enhance my life. In my banking job, I usually worked on Thursday nights until 8 pm. Since my son's preschool closed at six and I didn't have anyone in my immediate circle to look after him during that gap, I asked my employer if, on a temporary basis, I could finish at five in order to pick up my son in time, until I could find a reliable babysitter. While I explored different options to try to find one, my little voice kept telling me that something else would happen. A few weeks later, I found out that the government sent letters to all parents with children at my son's preschool announcing that it would be closing down the preschool by the end of December for its failure to comply with specific security requirements.

The school director hired a lawyer to plead her case in court. While we waited for the judge's verdict, I had to find an alternative place for my son to go to school, and I couldn't wait until the last minute in case his preschool was forced to close. Even if I found another preschool nearby, I would still have to find someone to look after my son on Thursday nights, and I did not feel comfortable hiring a stranger to care for him. I talked with my ex-boyfriend to see if we could consider the possibility of reversing guardianship roles temporarily for a few months. This implied that, as of the new year, my son would live on a full-time basis with his father, and I would see him on weekends. He was open to the idea, and made the necessary arrangements to enlist our son in a preschool facility close to his home to finish the school year. We agreed that for the following school year, we would reevaluate the situation.

After having my son under my full-time care for almost three years, I was heart-broken to go through this change, and saddened to find myself all alone in the big house we had just moved into. In the beginning, I had a hard time adjusting. I missed him so much. I felt like I had abandoned him and disrupted his stable routine. I was torn between feelings of guilt and solitude. Then I realized that this was a blessing in disguise. I started to see the other side of the coin; that this was actually a God-given opportunity for me to take advantage of this time to focus intensely on the development of my coaching business. By having greater flexibility in my schedule, I would be able to work with more clients, increase my income, and plan my exit from the banking world, perhaps sooner than spring season. By the time my son's father and I were to revisit our guardianship agreement, I might be completely self-employed, which meant I would no longer work on Thursday nights and I could have my son with me full-time again. Opportunities are everywhere all the time. It is just a matter of becoming aware of them and deciding to focus on what is to be gained rather than lost.

I want my accomplishments to be an inspiration for my son, to make him realize that all his dreams are possible. As he is in the early stages of his life, his subconscious mind is still pure and very receptive to the assimilation of new information. To maximize his wellbeing and encourage his full emancipation, I want to pass on to him the wonderful principles that we teach at LifeSuccess. Knowing how powerful his mind is and understanding that he can achieve anything he conceives of will be the crowning jewels of his success in life.

Another discovery I have made relates to why people don't have what they want in life. The majority of people trust neither themselves, their intuitive sense, a higher wisdom, nor that little voice. You can tell when your intuition strikes because you will feel inspired, and the obvious answer may suddenly present itself. There will be a feeling of unison and your insight may reach beyond the realm of logic.

Responsibility

You alone are responsible for your thoughts, feelings, actions, and, ultimately, your success. A balanced and fulfilled life doesn't just happen, and once you've acknowledged this fact, you can create the life you've always wanted. How do you feel each morning? Along with gaining awareness, you must also accept complete responsibility for your thoughts and outcomes. The solution to solving your problems is to take responsibility. Too many people do not take responsibility for the results that they produce. It is always other external factors that are to blame. "I can't be successful because my parents didn't pay for my education," or, "I'd weigh less if I had time to work out" are common statements made by people who fail to take responsibility.

Taking personal responsibility affects all aspects of our lives. We must also take full ownership of meeting our own needs, whether on the physical, mental, emotional, financial or spiritual level. When we depend on others to talk or act in ways that satisfy our needs, we set ourselves up for disappointment.

Believe it or not, when we take responsibility for the current circumstances that we have brought into our life, our life can then start to take new direction. Our life dramatically improves when we take responsibility. We cannot control other people and what they think and do, but we can control our own thoughts and actions, and that is where our personal power truly lies.

I have come to understand that many different people will cross our path during our lifetime, and the role they come to play is not to fill our emptiness, but to point us in the right direction so that we can fill it ourselves. I used to rely on other people to get what I needed.

For instance, I expected my boyfriends to love me in a specific way or my friends to behave according to certain standards. Whenever they didn't meet my expectations, I would blame them for treating me unfairly. They then reacted by saying that my expectations were unrealistic, or that I was being unreasonable or selfish. Of course, I did not like to hear that. I had the tendency to play the victim and sometimes lay guilt trips.

I spent a good part of my life being unhappy in my relationships because I felt caught in a vicious cycle. On the one hand, I was dependent on others in many respects to build my self-worth. Although I projected an image of success and confidence, inside I felt the total opposite. For example, if someone liked me, I liked myself. If another didn't, I second-guessed myself. If someone agreed with me, I felt great. If another criticized my ideas, I discounted the value of my ideas.

On the other hand, I knew there was a void in me. I did not know how to fill it myself, to learn to create my own happiness regardless of what other people thought or said. Whenever a disagreement would occur in the past, I automatically assumed that I was the one at fault. Some friendships came to an end due to unresolved conflicts, and I was deeply hurt by that. I could simply not handle rejection and abandonment; they were my worst fears. In his book *Aspire*, Kevin Hall talks about the definition of the word "friend." Hall defines it as "free".

I will never forget this. I want the people that I interact with to feel free with me as much as I want to feel free with them. By being free, there is no more room for fear in my relationships.

For many years, I tried to solve the big mystery of my life: why was I constantly stuck in the same unhealthy relationship patterns? It took me a long time to realize that the problem was not everyone else. The problem was me. I had incorrectly assumed that other people were responsible for meeting my needs, and believed that my happiness was based on gaining their acceptance. I had unwittingly created the hardships I experienced. I have since learned that there is only one person in control of what I think, feel, and do, and that is me. Blaming other people or circumstances for my misery was futile.

Today, I accept my mistakes and am letting go of the past. I cannot change what happened, but I can start creating a better life for myself. I am learning to fulfill my own needs by myself. If I want love, respect and harmony in my relationships, I must first and foremost love, respect and be in harmony with myself.

I have come to understand that relationships are not about meeting each other's needs; they are about sharing and growing together in mutual support. Responsibility is the greatest gift I have given myself, because it allowed me to liberate myself from the confines of my mental prison. No more dependency, guilt, manipulation, blame and shame. By being fully responsible for my needs, I no longer put myself in a position of waiting for someone else and risking the possibility of them hurting or betraying me.

By gaining humility, developing our inspiration and intuition, and taking responsibility, we will be able to use resources from past experiences that allow us to make better decisions. Don't let fear get in the way of developing these three important items. Fear is a powerful force keeping us from moving forward. Learning to incorporate these traits into our life guides us to make decisions that we thought we could never make before. In the space below, list a few areas of your life where you can incorporate humility, hone your inspiration and intuition and take more responsibility.

Humility	Inspiration/ Intuition	Responsibility

Chapter 8 Summary

A Whole New World

• Humility is what brings the right balance into our lives.

• By opening our mind and becoming compassionate and nonjudgmental, we can reach heights of success we never imagined.

• We are spiritual beings gifted with an intellect and living in a physical body.

• We must not limit our goals and dreams to what we can perceive through our physical senses only.

• When we take responsibility for the circumstances that we have created, our life can start to take new direction.

Chapter 9

Conquer the War Within

Chapter 9

Conquer the War Within

One of my favorite quotes is, "If I want to be free, I've got to be me. Not the me I think my wife thinks I should be, not the me I think my kids think I should be. I have got to be me." We must disassociate ourselves from other people's opinions and judgments because we have no control over what they think. We only have control over what we think.

There is no better reward than freedom because it means we have totally outgrown our deficiencies and limitations. We recognize that the answers to our problems reside within. We have a clear picture of our mind and we comprehend the role that each part plays in the creation of our results. We understand the power of our thoughts and choose them with higher awareness. We give energy to ideas that improve the quality of our lives. We dare to dream and live in the light of our immense potential. We know that by impressing thoughts and ideas which bring about the manifestation of prosperity. We alter how we feel, and by acting upon those feelings we create results that are in harmony with what we think about. We are in sync. In no way, shape or form do we wait for people or circumstances to change in order to create our happiness because we know that all the resources we need already lie within us.

When we conquer the war within, all influences from the outside world—friends, family, the media—cease to dictate what we should think, how we should feel and how we should act. We agree that we are totally responsible for our thoughts, feelings and actions. As a result, we no longer feel the need to blame people or circumstances for our shortcomings. We cease to try to control things or people that are beyond our control. We realize that taking risks is part of life. We open ourselves to new ideas and break out of our comfort zone because we believe doing so is essential to our evolution and personal development. We continually nurture a greater awareness in relation to the spiritual side of our beings, and master our ability to think before we act. We believe in our greatness, and we confidently walk along a path of endless growth.

Placing Distance

In pursuing my journey in personal development, I am learning to live my life according to what I think is best for me. Sometimes, this implies that I must distance myself from people who do not agree with the path I am taking. Placing distance does not mean becoming indifferent to them as people. It simply means detaching from their opinions and judgments. This way, I do not give anyone the power to influence my decisions and the course of my life. From now on, I stand by what I think without feeling the need to seek approval or please others. For me, this is self-respect and the ticket to freedom.

How we define ourselves is often the direct result of what other people say and think about us. One of the primary reasons we are so concerned with others' opinions of us is because we want their approval. Why is it that we have this underlying need to seek approval from those closest to us? Recently, I initiated a get-together with a friend so that I could ask for his help. This person has seen my evolution since my enrollment in the LifeSuccess training program. He has been very happy with my progress so far and believes in my potential for launching a successful coaching practice. I hired him to design my personal website at a very expensive price. I believed that he was the right person for the job, and we developed a reliable strategy to promote my business on the internet. Everything was working well until I returned from my training in Florida.

When I came back, I excitedly told him all about the events of the summit and the incredible news that I had decided to write a book. He listened and was happy for me, but was taken aback by the investment the book represented in time and in money. Since my return from Florida, I have been very busy writing my book and getting ready to move, and as a result, the website design had not progressed any further. During our meal, my friend asked me for an update on the latest news in my life. He knew about my recent move and my decision to keep my job for a few more months.

I told him I thought I was doing well, especially given that I was managing so many things simultaneously.

However, I expressed to him that I had spent a considerable amount of money on the website, on top of my personal development training, and admitted that I was beginning to feel increasing pressure from being financially overstretched. I was starting to panic. I wanted to discuss with him the possibility of putting the website on hold, and see if I could get back a portion of the consulting fee I paid him upfront when I accepted his contract. The amount covered his fees for a period of twelve months and, at present, a portion of it was being unused since no work was being done on the website. In addition, many pages were still incomplete and it was not providing me with any income. Unfortunately, our discussion did not turn out the way I had hoped.

My friend was very puzzled by my situation. He did not understand why I decided to get involved with a book contract. He thought I was taking on too many projects at the same time, and that I had derailed from my initial strategy, which was to build a personal website and use it as a tool to promote my coaching services and gradually grow a client base. He asked me questions which made me feel even worse, such as, "How will you be able to increase your business income now that you decided to keep your job longer? How much longer will you stay at your job? Why did you decide to do the book now? What if it does not work? How do you explain why you took on so much? Why is it that you are coaching people to go after their dreams and leave their comfort zone while you are not doing it yourself?" His questions demonstrated the confusion he was feeling from my sudden change in business strategy.

He did not think that writing this book was a priority at this current time in my life. In fact, he did not really believe that it would be an asset in helping me develop my business, at least in the short term. To him, it would just be a book that people would read and that's it. I was starting to feel incompetent and irresponsible, that I lacked good judgment in my decisions, had taken on insurmountable pressure, and had put my financial future at risk. Even if I was enjoying the experience of writing my book, I was no longer convinced that this book was a good thing, and I began to doubt that the investment would pay off. I was overwhelmed with negative emotions. I even seriously questioned my ability to reason well and manage my life properly. I let myself be totally consumed by what my friend was thinking.

When our lunch was over, I drove back to work. Feelings of guilt, torment and regret took over me. I became extremely anxious, to the point of indigestion. I could not bear the thought of my friend discrediting my book project and making me feel that I was not practicing what I was preaching. Back in my office, I could not concentrate. I could not work efficiently. I kept asking myself "What have I gotten myself into? Have I completely lost my mind?" I thought to myself, "Here I am writing a book about fear and I cannot even manage my own." I was in terrible distress. I had to do something and fast. I decided to call my friend Regina to talk. She was out for lunch. I sent her an email asking her to call me as soon as possible. Every minute that passed felt like an eternity.

While waiting for her call, I focused my attention on two specific chapters in Bob Proctor's bestselling book, *You Were Born Rich: Let Go and Let God* and *Expect an Abundance.*

I needed to calm my mind and shift gears in my thinking. Immersing myself back into some of the key principles he teaches, like seeing ourselves already in the possession of the good we desire, and believing that whatever we need to materialize our goals will occur at the right time, was extremely effective in reducing the stress I was under. The book also reminded me that we are spiritual beings and that our body is an instrument through which an infinite supply of energy flows.

Take the example of a light bulb. Depending on the number of watts, a light bulb will emit light at different intensities, even if the source of the electrical current is always the same. Using this analogy, our bodies are comparable to the light bulb, and our thoughts to the number of watts. The infinite supply of energy flows to and through our body at an intensity that corresponds to the frequency of our thoughts. In other words, when we focus on worry, doubt and fear, we choose thoughts of low frequency that restrain the intensity of energy that can flow through our body. On the other hand, when we focus on thoughts of faith, abundance, and joy, we entertain thoughts of a higher frequency which increase the intensity of energy flowing through our body. The higher the frequency, the more we can attract other thoughts of the same frequency. Reading these chapters changed my vibration and as a result, I felt calmer.

Half an hour later, Regina called back. I explained to her what happened with my friend and how I was feeling after our encounter. It was so good to connect with a like-minded person. Regina was very understanding and said to me, "Lorie, I will be blunt and honest with you. You cannot let yourself be affected by what other people think. At times, there are people who can be negative influences in your life and you can't let them get to you like this." She went on to say that writing this book is an amazing accomplishment in my life. She reminded me that the book was only a three-month commitment, as I plan to launch it at the final LifeSuccess training event, which will be held live. Regina reassured me that now was the best time to write my book because my coaching business had not yet grown to a point where it was time-consuming. Later on it would be infinitely more challenging for me to find the time to write a book, to the point where I might be tempted to drop the project altogether, and let the opportunity of a lifetime pass by. I realized that she was entirely right. Regina asked me if writing this book was something I felt good about, and I said yes, absolutely. Not only do I feel right about writing this book, I am living proof that I am facing my fears head on and living what I teach as a personal development coach.

I drew two huge lessons from this story: first, to persist with my projects regardless of what other people think, and second, to stick to my gut feelings. As much as I knew that I should always follow my instinct, there was a part of me that tended to deviate from this truth in practice because I let myself be side-tracked by outside influences. Now I know that to accomplish my goals, my inner voice is always the best counsel.

We must keep in mind friends and family members will not necessarily cope well with the changes we are making. They are entitled to their opinion and are free to strongly disagree with the changes we are undergoing, but we must not let their views become a reason to doubt or abandon our goals. More importantly, we must not let it affect the opinion we have of ourselves. When others attempt to talk "sense" into us, we should try to understand the cause of their reaction. Could it be their own fears coming to the surface? Could they be scared to lose us or afraid they will lose control over us? Or, could it be that a mirror is put in their face showing them that we are growing while they are not?

No matter what the cause is, it is important to remain strong and to stay committed to our goals. When the going gets tough, we must not be afraid to get tougher. Only we know what is best for ourselves.

Think of how much energy and time we waste on caring about what other people think. So why do we set ourselves up for failure by giving any credence to what they say? It is easier to look to the outside rather than face the fact that we have to take responsibility for our own lives. The truth is that it is more courageous to look deep inside ourselves, acknowledge our weaknesses, and take the steps necessary to correct them. Those brave enough to do so meet their full potential and are successful in their own right.

Can-Do Attitude

The reason that the need for external approval is so detrimental is that it gives other people control over our emotions. When others bombard us with bad advice and opinions, our self-esteem plummets. Happiness and fulfillment are internal, and when we rely on external sources that are critical or judgmental, we will develop feelings of negativity, and, inevitably, a bad attitude.

As our attitude sours, we will be subject to destructive thoughts and sabotaging self-talk. There is one aspect of our lives we have complete control over and that is our attitude. Attitude is everything and it differentiates the successful people from the unsuccessful ones. Attitude is the composite of our thoughts, feelings and actions. A person with a positive attitude is someone who chooses the right thoughts.

Inevitably, this person feels good and acts in ways that reflects their positive mindset. The person, consciously or unconsciously, understands the power of thought and, through faith, always expects a positive outcome. Should the end result not materialize as planned, the person takes the lesson and learns from it. When faith and understanding are the motors of our decisions and actions, there is no more room for fear.

We can truly transform our lives with a change in attitude. Henry Ford once said, "If you think you can do a thing or think you can't do a thing, you're right." The same can be said of attitude: if we believe we are great, then we are. We must believe this in order to accomplish our goals.

To build your self-esteem, you must overcome any fears, anxieties, self-doubts and limiting beliefs that you may have, such as "No I can't," or, "I'll never be smart or good enough to accomplish anything."

When I was transforming my attitude and was plagued with doubt, I focused on all of my good qualities and accomplishments. With repetition and practice, this process reversed my fear, anxiety and doubt, and helped me feel better about myself. After a couple of weeks, I found myself succeeding more often and felt better about my life. In the space following list your good qualities and accomplishments.

Good qualities	Accomplishments

When you find yourself saying "I can't," go back and review your list. Whenever we think about what we do well, it's a form of self-affirmation that builds self-esteem and reinforces our positive beliefs. We need to remind ourselves constantly about how great we are and what we are capable of doing so that we can have what we want. When was the last time you paid attention to your inner world and you listened to your positive inner voice?

I have a good friend from my years as a undergraduate in university. We periodically stayed in touch after graduation, and occasionally saw each other. Regardless of how often we spoke, she and I maintained a very good connection. She knows about my decision to pursue a career in coaching, and a few months ago, hosted a gathering at her house and invited me to present some of the concepts and principles we teach at LifeSuccess. There was quite a bit of interest generated by my speech, so much so that there were enough people interested in forming a Master Mind group. My friend was also interested in participating, but was unsure she had the time, since she had committed to finishing her doctorate thesis in the next few months. I urged her to join the group, and strongly believed inside that she would greatly benefit from group sessions. I have observed many people unlock their vast potential and be astounded by their results from one week to the next. I knew this could make an important difference in her life. She finally agreed to participate, and now after every session, she tells me that she is very happy with her decision.

It is imperative to shift our outlook from one of negativity to a constructive and encouraging attitude. A positive attitude is more important than our abilities when it comes to whether or not we'll be successful. A positive perception must be a part of our daily routine. If you have a persistent feeling that you are not good enough, smart enough, or capable enough, you need to evaluate your current attitude. The way we view the world and handle challenges impacts our entire life.

Embrace Your Mistakes

Each time a rocket soars into the sky toward the moon, it veers off-course almost 99% of the time. A rocket reaches the moon by readjusting its compass as it moves through space until it reaches its destination. Mistakes are our internal compass. They help us learn what not to do. Mistakes have resulted in some of the world's best inventions. Rarely does any sort of revolutionary medicinal cure or discovery reveal its full potential on the first try. Could you have ever imagined that mold could cure a sore throat? It does and it was found by accident. Penicillin was once nothing more than mold. Success is virtually impossible without experiencing a mistake or two first.

Our attitude toward mistakes is that we shouldn't make them because they are bad. I disagree completely. For instance, when I deal with clients in the financial world, I sometimes rely on too much jargon or assume that they understand everything I am presenting. There were a few times when that led the business relationship to turn sour because I would go out of my way to justify my recommendations. Occasionally, I felt comfortable enough with the client to ask him why we were unable to come to a mutual agreement.

The response would be that I was not providing the client with the privilege of being a client. One of the golden rules in business is that the client is always right and that was not how I made him feel. This made me realize that as employees working for large financial institutions, we sometimes lose sight of the basic principle of treating our clients the same way we would like to be treated. Should this situation happen again, I will adjust my approach rather than react defensively.

Mistakes are a necessary part of our learning process, and once you change your attitude to reflect that belief, you release your fear and step onto the path of happiness, success, and freedom. The next time you make a mistake, don't perceive it as the end of the world. Instead, change your attitude and think of it as valuable feedback for your future success. It is vital to accept our mistakes as essential lessons toward our personal and professional growth rather than hang on to them and beat ourselves up about something we did in the past.

Don't "shoulda, coulda, woulda" yourself into a frenzy. No matter how big the mistake is, just release it and move on. Mistakes aren't important, results are. Focus on what you can do the next time to get the results you want.

The best life lessons come when we are challenged and pushed beyond our comfort zone. Difficulties, mistakes, obstacles and hardships are many times a prelude to great feats. When we create a mindset that it is okay to make mistakes as long as we learn from them, we will have the confidence to work toward our goals no matter what happens.

Chapter 9 Summary

Conquer the War Within

• Answers to our problems reside within.

• When we conquer the war within, all influences from our outside world—friends, family and the media—no longer dictate what we think, how we feel, and how we act.

• How we define ourselves is often the direct result of what other people say and think about us.

• A positive attitude is more important than our abilities when it comes to whether or not we'll be successful.

• Mistakes are a necessary part of the learning process. Once we change our attitudes to reflect that belief, we release our fear and step onto the path of happiness, success, and freedom.

Chapter 10

Freedom! The Other Side of Fear

Chapter 10

Freedom! The Other Side of Fear

When we start enjoying the fruits of greater freedom, we see our lives change for the better in many ways. We feel we are elevating in altitude. We feel strong and motivated. We want to conquer the world and challenge ourselves even more. Just when we think we have reached great strides in creating a new life for ourselves, someone or something takes us off track.

Depending on the nature of the person or event, we may realign ourselves quickly and move on. Or, we may slide back into our old habits and lose what we had gained thus far. Our emotions can get in the way, and next thing we know, we feel like we are back to square one.

It is an inescapable fact that life is composed of a series of risks. If we spend our entire life in our comfort zone, we will never move forward. Every action we take involves risk, and there will be times that we fail. Following my meeting with my website designer, I came to realize that it was time to reflect on the future of our business relationship. I want my personal website to be an extension of myself, and I believe it is important to work with a web designer whose strategy and energy are in harmony with mine. As our respective visions were diverging, I made the decision to end our business relationship.

I walked away with an unfinished website that cost me several thousand dollars. As I did not know much about web design, I took a risk, thinking that my investment would bring the final outcome I expected. It didn't. I am responsible for all of my decisions; I chose to learn a valuable lesson from this and move on. I do not see this experience as a failure. I still believe in my website project, and I will accomplish it with someone else. There is no guarantee in anything that we do in life, but that does not mean that we should let setbacks stop us.

The fear of failure is often the primary factor preventing us from accomplishing our goals and fulfilling our dreams. As a result of this fear, many people don't do anything. Procrastination is far riskier than taking action. Too many people don't go after what they want and allow fear to creep in and steal their dreams. The truth of the matter is that we can't achieve anything if we just sit around and wait for life to happen. We are the only ones who can truly make our lives better. Nobody is going to do it for us. That's not how life works.

How about you? What is fear preventing you from doing in your life? How much better would your life be if you could relinquish your fears? Anytime we step into the unknown and take a chance, some sort of adversity will accompany the risk. You must be ready to face adversity and deal with problems or obstacles that present themselves along the way. Two of the natural byproducts of any type of fear are doubt and a lack of faith. Once we release our fear, the happier we become, the more fulfilled we are, and the better our life journey becomes.

Push Out Doubt

Doubt is nothing more than a lack of faith in ourselves and our abilities. When we doubt ourselves, we instigate an inner tug of war. We badly want to do something new, but we are pulled back by doubt. Have you ever had of an idea and felt motivated and excited by it at first, but as time passed, start feeling a resounding sense of "I can't do that"? If you answered yes, then you've succumbed to doubt and started to rationalize yourself out of a dream. As we learned in the previous chapter, we shouldn't let anyone else talk us out of our dreams, so there is no reason in the world to convince ourselves to stop trying to achieve them.

Our subconscious minds have been set for certain levels of success or results based on our past experiences and programming. That's why when we back off or quit because of fear, anxiety and doubt, we're not telling ourselves, "I'm not going to do that because I'm afraid." Instead, we give ourselves a list of excuses like, "I can't do it," or "It's no use, it won't work anyway." Every excuse you can think of will surface—and quickly—because these paradigms have been living in our minds for a very long time.

You might even try to rationalize your way out of your aspirations by convincing yourself that your current situation, your job, for instance, isn't that bad after all. Rationalizing keeps you in your comfort zone. Your life might not be much more than rote and routine. Instead of truly being fulfilled, your life is a habit. Rather than really living, you stay where you are comfortable. If you grew up "programmed" to doubt yourself, more than likely you will sabotage any goals you want to accomplish before you even begin! Through doubt, you attract what you don't want. The choice is yours. You don't have to give doubt a reason to exist. Make the choice to reject it and allow yourself to become emotionally involved with your goals. Know this: life will continually test you. Doubt can resurface from time to time and we cannot completely eliminate fear. However, we can learn to be better at overcoming it. There are many practical things we can do to stay in control and keep ourselves on top of the situation.

I certainly went through a few important relapses recently. When I decided to extend my employment a few more months, I went through an intense period of mixed emotions. I felt some relief in delaying my target date and doing so significantly reduced my stress level. It also allowed me to concentrate on my physical wellbeing because I was nearing exhaustion.

However, I felt like a failure afterward and I was not proud of myself. It was as if I had denied my ability to meet the initial target date and had stopped having faith that I could successfully make the leap into the entrepreneurial world. I felt like I had grabbed a security blanket and retreated back into my comfort zone.

The move into my new house was also getting closer, so I had even less time at my disposal to participate in post-training activities with LifeSuccess, to be in regular contact with my colleagues, to continue my self-study, and to develop more business opportunities in individual and group coaching. My immediate responsibilities meant that I could not invest as much time practicing my newly-acquired skills, nor could I earn more income through my coaching business. I began to feel the distance growing between myself and my new world with LifeSuccess. I felt more and more withdrawn. Whenever I was struck by frustration or fear, I felt that my mental toughness in maintaining a positive outlook was crumbling. My old conditioning took over. My feelings regressed to worry, doubt, and fear. I experienced high anxiety on a regular basis. I felt overwhelmed with many substantial projects going on simultaneously. I suffered from sleep deprivation and weight loss. I was progressively losing control.

Thankfully, there were two things that kept me from falling into depression. The first one was writing this book. As I kept advancing each chapter, I would totally disconnect from my current reality and plunge myself back into the LifeSuccess principles I am so passionate about. Understanding the mind, and learning and applying how we can choose to live a more fulfilling life are the concepts that I held onto to get through this challenging period of my life. Every time a negative thought would come to mind, I would immediately stop myself and become aware that I could choose a more positive and constructive thought. Almost instantaneously, I felt better because I released the weight of the negative thought and replaced it with the uplifting feeling of the positive thought.

We are what we think about. Therefore when we change what we think, we change how we feel. When we feel good, we produce positive results. As I was writing, I was entertaining thoughts of accomplishment, alignment with purpose, contribution to society, and success. As a result, I felt joy, gratitude, fulfillment and self-growth. As such, I was able to focus my mind on the wonderful triumphs on the horizon rather than the temporary challenges I was currently facing. My mentor Bob Proctor says that when we are out of our comfort zone, we are facing the unknown, and this causes us to feel varying degrees of nervousness and fear. However, this is a sign that we are actually on the right path because it means we are giving ourselves an opportunity to grow. Growth implies risk. When we stay in our comfort zone and make safe choices all the time, we stop growing.

The other positive event was settling into my new home. As much as the move was a laborious process, I felt it allowed me to leave many parts of my old life behind. My old apartment had become a reflection of my old self and my old belief system. Although it was a convenient and acceptable place to live in, it did not really reflect the kind of abundant lifestyle I now wanted for myself and my son. To me, my new home is an embodiment of comfort, spaciousness, style, elegance, warmth and opulence. It provides an atmosphere of intimacy, pleasure, serenity and inspiration. I am immersed in nature. Trees, mountains, lakes and a wide selection of species surround me. Living in this environment brings me peace of mind and heightened creativity. I feel blessed to have this special place as my home. I am surrounded by so much abundance in this house that I cannot help but feel abundant. I look forward to filling it with many precious memories.

There is magnificence in this world, and you are entitled to it. Whatever you want, you deserve. You can have it. You don't want to go through life making "what if" statements. Fill your life with "when?" statements instead. If you feel the need to doubt something, then doubt your limits. Get out there and start living the life you want!

The Ultimate Weapons

Integrating new paradigms will take less time than the years you have been maintaining your old paradigms. You must be the master of your mind. Repetition and faith are your ultimate weapons. It is important to understand that the transformation that occurs within when we change our thinking patterns is a continual process that never ends. It is a journey, not a final destination. We must keep in mind that all along, we are challenging the old thinking habits that have been deeply entrenched in our minds for years. Now that we want to replace them with new thoughts, ones that will serve us better, our old paradigms put up a fight. They do not want to be kicked out. They have been so comfortable in the deeply rooted seat of our subconscious mind and they won't disappear at the snap of our fingers.

When we face adversity and doubt, we must change our interpretation of those experiences. Instead of interpreting a problem or challenge as insurmountable, we need to have faith and translate it into a positive thought process. To replace our paradigms, we have to eliminate their impact. You may have just read that and thought, "What! I'll never be able to completely get rid of them." Do you detect doubt in that thought process? Any thought embedded into the subconscious can be removed and replaced through repetition and faith.

Since we formed our current beliefs and habits by hearing them repeatedly when we were young it makes sense that we can replace them with repetition as well. The primary method to reprogram your subconscious mind is through deliberate repetition of the new beliefs you want. Repetition "plants" a thought in your subconscious mind and new beliefs sprout only after they've been repeated enough times. These thoughts and beliefs continue to strengthen with further repetition and begin to take root. To plant a new belief, you have to make a conscious effort to think in positive terms for 30 days until this way of thinking becomes a habit.

Reprogramming your subconscious mind can be done through visualizations and affirmations. I visualize and affirm good thoughts every day. A good way to start to reprogram your mind is to practice visualizations of what you want and repeat positive affirmations at least 10 minutes a day three times a day. For instance, visualize and affirm when you first wake up, again at lunch, and before you go to bed at night. This routine must be done daily for at least 30 days. If you miss a day, it is okay. As a matter of fact it is fairly common. Just remember each time you miss just one day of reprogramming your subconscious mind, you have to start your count back to day 1. After 30 consecutive days of thinking new thoughts and planting new beliefs, you will quickly notice your attitude shift and see more and more success in the areas you've been visualizing and affirming.

Alongside the many facets of fear that I expressed in the stories that I shared throughout this book, there is one area where I never let fear be in command, and that is in regards to the quality of my work as a coach. In previous occupations, my low self-confidence was sometimes an issue that affected my work. With my new vocation, I did not want to perpetuate this trend. It is amazing how, by simply repeating to myself daily that I am adding value to people's lives, it became a habitual thought pattern that consequently was reflected in my results. I received outstanding compliments from some of the coaching clients I worked with, such as, "My life has changed since I met you," "You helped me identify the cause of a major block and because of that, I feel alive again," or, "You helped me change my focus in life." Do not underestimate the power of repetition to create new thinking habits. It will change your life.

Next, let's look at the other ultimate weapon of faith. In his book *Think and Grow Rich*, Napoleon Hill names faith as the second of thirteen steps to a prosperous life. He calls faith "the head chemist of the mind." In order for us to challenge our belief systems and release our fear, we have to have faith. Faith is the belief and complete trust in something for which there is no proof, something believed with strong conviction and envisioned as a certainty. The majority of people aren't comfortable with trusting the unknown. They prefer to base their decisions and actions only on what is rational, objective and fact-based. The problem with this line of thinking is that it is based on habits. People prefer to stay in their comfort zone and work only on what is familiar to them.

Lately in my life, I have come to recognize the significance of faith in my understanding and acceptance of the Universal Laws, especially the Law of Cause and Effect which states that what you give, you get back. At my last banking job, I was hired to fill a new position and I was assigned a portfolio of clients. During the first year, I spent a lot of time getting to know my clients and sowing seeds for future business development. After eight months on the job, I was far from reaping the results I was expecting. So I tried harder. I made more calls, I sent presentation letters and I kept having faith that one day, my efforts would pay off. Just before the end of the business year, new opportunities arose to close on large investments and sign important transfers.

I have for a long time been fascinated by faith and how to build it. When I decided to completely change my career, I had to choose between adjusting my goals and lowering my expectations, or moving forward in absolute faith that I would reach my goals. By completely immersing myself in faith, I received clarity and a much deeper understanding of faith. A strong faith will nurture you and shield you from circumstances and outside turmoil. There are always external forces working in our lives, and our level of faith determines how we perceive and handle them. For us to have true faith, we need to surrender our logic, reason and need for control to move forward. For me, faith has been one of the most important factors contributing to the success I now experience. Faith enables us to release all fear and find freedom.

When pursuing our goals, we must to go outside of our comfort zone and live on faith. I know it may seem difficult to simply trust that everything will work out, which is why faith has to be backed up with strong unwavering belief that you are living on purpose.

We all have unlimited potential and we just need to have the faith to pursue our purpose. We are all a unique part of the divine, all knowing and all powerful. Our current results are a reflection of our efforts, not of our potential. The goals and dreams we have are within our reach. We just have to have the faith to stick our arm out. We must surrender our fear and accept that there are concepts that we don't understand. Moving into unknown territory can feel a bit chaotic, uncomfortable and overwhelming, but with faith we can let go of our fears and trust we are on the right path.

We only have one life, and none of us know if it's going to be short or long. Make the most of what you are given. We all have talents, gifts, and uniqueness. Our obligation is to accept these gifts and spend our lives sharing our gifts with the world. When we come from a place of growth and abundance, we celebrate others' success. Help other people to succeed and reach their goals. I would like to offer a special thanks to three people who have helped me grow and who brought water to the well in terms of stories to share as I wrote this book.

Rick, you are truly a dear friend and you will forever have a unique place in my heart. You are an incredible person, and I have learned a lot from you and your accomplishments. I appreciate that our relationship has at times traveled a bumpy road, and I value that we experienced some tension from time to time. I understand that since my involvement with LifeSuccess, you have come to question some of my choices and decisions. I realize that I am taking a path that is very unfamiliar to you.

You know that I am one to finish what I start and succeed at everything I decide to undertake. I have faith that you will be my biggest fan and we will have many cheerful moments to celebrate together. Thank you for every caring thought, kind word, and supporting action that you have contributed to my life.

Tania, I greatly admire you for your moral strength and your ability to deeply touch people's lives in many different ways. You are an inspiration for your tenacity in overcoming deep inner battles and searching for the light. I appreciate your talking to me with gentleness and an open heart and for making me aware of different ways that I can become a better person. I believe that if you are able to see greatness in others, it is because you also have it in yourself. Thank you for your presence and honesty.

Regina, you have been the guiding light of my ship throughout this journey. Discovering the author in me has indeed been a beautiful gift, but an even more valuable one is the pleasure of having crossed paths with you. I will always be grateful to you and I look forward to the unfolding of a prosperous and authentic relationship for many more years to come. Thank you for lending an open ear and walking by my side while I experienced many life-altering moments in writing this book.

Other people's successes don't take anything away from our success. I operate from a plane of creativity rather than competition. Competition is a long standing belief that the universe is limited and inspires fear. Just imagine how much more freedom we would have to express ourselves and follow our dreams if we came from a platform of abundance and believed that there was more than enough for everyone.

I came to understand that, although freedom is the ultimate way we should live our lives, the price to pay to get it is quite high. I recently came across the following quote: "Freedom is not free." These words speak loudly and truthfully. It is important to realize that to achieve freedom, it means that we travel in the opposite direction of how we have been programmed. We do not follow the masses anymore and we encounter great resistance from people in our immediate circle who are used to our old selves. Resistance to change, obstacles and challenges are undeniable requirements for growth; remaining within the boundaries of our comfort zone would simply impede progress. It is not always easy and enjoyable to politely turn our backs on people who disagree with our new way of life, but whose life is it?

Every day, I fill my mind with beautiful and empowering thoughts. I understand that whatever I want to create in my life, I must have the thought in mind before it can manifest into reality. I repeat positive affirmations which make me feel vibrant, joyful and enthusiastic. These feelings push me to continually take inspired action, moving me closer to the realization of my dreams. I create results that I want. I am in control. I love my life and I savor the fruits of my accomplishments. I see each new day as an opportunity to enjoy the magic of the present moment and I express gratitude for all the good that life has to offer. I am on my way to becoming mentally, emotionally, physically, financially and spiritually free!

Chapter 10 Summary

Freedom! The Other Side of Fear

• If we spend our entire life in our comfort zone, we will never move forward.

• Procrastination is far riskier than taking action.

• Through doubt, we attract what we don't want.

• The more we release our fears, the happier we become, the more fulfilled we are, and the better our life journey gets.

• The success of others doesn't take anything away from our success.

LaVergne, TN USA
16 March 2011
220412LV00002B/1/P